TURKEY

Ali Kılıçkaya
Archaeologist

SILK ROAD
PUBLICATIONS

CONTENTS

INTRODUCTION

Turkey, the junction between Asia and Europe continents, has witnessed many civilizations through the ages as it is situated on the passageway of nations throughout history and it is located on a land, both with a strategic position and also all required geographical conditions for subsistence of people. Anatolia has been settled since Old Stone Age. Archaeological excavations show that first settlements in Anatolia go back to B.C. 10.500 years.

Being a stage for many civilizations, such as Hittite, Phrygia, Urartu, Lydia, Ion, Caria, Lycia, Hellenistic, Roman, Byzantine, Anatolian Seljuk and Ottoman, down the ages, Turkey is known as "Country of Civilizations". It is in the position of outdoor museum thanks to its rich historical and cultural inheritance. It ranks among the richest countries of the world with its cultural and natural beauties. There is a different history and culture in each region and corner of the country.

Turkey has the most famous cities of ancient times such as Ephesus, Aphrodisias, Perge, Miletus, Priene, Hierapolis; Pamukkale, which is unique natural wonder of the world, and fascinating Cappadocia, Museum-city Mardin; world's cultural city Istanbul; East Black Sea Region's Flatlands and Mountains, which are are compared with Alps. Furthermore, Turkey is a country, which has shores, long beaches, witnessing "Blue Cruises" and famous with unspoiled green nature with its lacy cove, waterside thicket and bays, rich thermal springs, land, surrounded by sea on its three sides and with four seasons at the same time and also hospitable people.

Assos

GEOGRAPHICAL POSITION OF TURKEY

Turkey territories, located between 36° - 42° Northern parallels and 26° - 45° Eastern meridians in the northern hemisphere, is situated on Asian and European continents. Turkey territories, located in Asian continent, are called Anatolia and its territories, located in European continent, are called Thrace. Anatolia is a Greek word and means "eastern country", "the place where sun rises". Furthermore, Anatolia was called "Asia Minor" in the antique age. Istanbul and Çanakkale Straits and Sea of Marmara divide territories of the country into two parts. Moreover, three sides of the country are surrounded with Black Sea, Aegean Sea and Mediterranean Sea. Its surface area is 776 723 square kilometers and population of the country is about 72 millions. It is a mosaic with folk, composed of various ethnical origin people such as Turkish, Kurdish, Armenian, Greek, Arabian, Bosnian, Georgian, Laz, Circassian, Albanian, Azerbaijani, Chechen etc. Although vast majority of peoples are Muslim, there are also people, believing in Christian and Jewish religion. Its capital city is Ankara. Republic of Turkey is a democratic, laic, social law state. It is bordered with Georgia, Armenia, Nakhichevan (Azerbaijan) and Iran in the east; Syria and Iraq in the south; Greece and Bulgaria countries in the west. Turkey is divided into seven geographical regions. Marmara Region, located on two continents, is a region which has moderate altitudes in terms of surface features. It has productive lowlands such as Bursa, Sakarya, Ergene. Sun flower, olive, tobacco, grape, rice, corn, are the means of living for people. Region is the most developed region of Turkey in terms of economy. Its climate is hot and arid in summer and mild and rainy in winter. Mountains run perpendicular to the sea in Aegean Region and shores are very recessed and protrusive. Bakırçayı, Gediz, Küçük Menderes and Büyük Menderes rivers irrigate the productive lowlands, on which they pass. Grape, fig, cotton, olive, tobacco, are the means of living for people. Region's climate is hot and arid in summer and mild and rainy in winter. Taurus Mountains, located in the Mediterranean Region, run parallel to the sea; there are productive lowlands such as Antalya, Çukurova and Amik. Its climate is hot and arid in summer and mild and rainy in winter. Its vegetation cover is composed of maquis and forests. Cotton, citrus fruits, banana, and vegetable production are the means of living of people. Greenhousing is very developed. Antalya and its surroundings are in the position of tourism center. Central Anatolia Region is covered with steppes. Agriculture and animal breeding are the means of living of people. Kızılırmak, the longest river of Turkey, reaches to Black Sea archly within the region. Konya lowland, which is the biggest lowland and wheat silo of Turkey, and Salt Lake, which is the second biggest lake, are located in this region. This region is moderate mountainy and its climate is hot and arid in summer and cold in winter and it has a continental climate. Northern Anatolian Mountains, located in Black Sea Region, run parallel to the sea. There are productive Çarşamba and Bafra lowlands in the coasts, where Kızılırmak and Yeşilırmak rivers reach to the sea. Eastern Black Sea Region is usually rainy in every season. Mountains are covered with forests. Tea, corn, hazelnut, tobacco are the means of living of people. Eastern Anatolia Region is the mountainiest region of the country and is composed of high mountains and plateaus. Mount Ararat, the highest mountain of Turkey and Lake Van, the biggest lake, are located in this region. Fırat and Dicle Rivers go out from this region and reach to the sea outside boundaries of the country. Its climate is hot in summer and cold in winter and it has a continental climate. Agriculture and animal breeding are the means of living of people. Agriculture and animal breeding are the means of living of people in Southeastern Anatolia Region, which is the Region of Dams. Wheat, lentil, cotton, pistachio, grape are the main agricultural products. Main oil reservoirs of Turkey are located in this region. This region is moderate mountainy and its climate is hot in summer and cold in winter.

A BRIEF HISTORY OF TURKEY

These lands in Anatolia have been settled since 12 500 years. The oldest settlement belongs to Old Stone Age (Paleolithic Age) and it dates back B.C. 10 500 and it is found in Göbeklitepe in Şanlıurfa. New Stone Age settlements are seen in Diyarbakır Çayönü, Konya Çatalhöyük and Burdur Hacılar between B.C. 8000-5500 years. Anatolia had Copper Age between B.C. 5500-3000 years and; Bronze Age between B.C. 3000-1200 years and Iron Age between B.C. 1200-750 years.

Istanbul Archeology Museum

Aşıklı Tumulus-Aksaray

We know about Hatti Civilization, which is the first known civilization in Anatolia from sources of Hittite, establishing the first state in Anatolia between B.C. 1660 and B.C. 1190 years and having capital city, named as Hattusas. Script is used in Anatolia firstly in the period of Assyrian Trading colonies (B.C. 1950-1750). Hittites also start to use the script as of 1600 and becomes the first state, using the script in Anatolia. Phrygians establish a state with capital city, named as Gordion and with the headquarter in the triangle of Afyon, Eskisehir, Ankara between B.C. 750-300 years. We see Urartu Civilization, with capital city, named as Tushpa and with the headquarter in the triangle of Van, Erzincan and Erivan between B.C. 860-580 years in Eastern Anatolia. Besides Troy Civilization (B.C. 3000-1200) in Western Anatolia, Ion Civilization and Lydia, Caria and Lycia Civilizations are seen between B.C. 700-300. Various states and kingdoms reign in Anatolia between B.C. 323-30 years. Romans, existing in Anatolia since B.C. 2nd Century, have control over Anatolia completely beginning from B.C. 30 years. After Roman Empire was divided in A.D. 395, we see East Roman Empire in Anatolia. Central Asian Turks start to come to Anatolia by beginning from middle of 9th Century. We see that Anatolian Seljuk State is established in 1078 with capital city, named as Nicaea, and Ottoman Beylic is established in 1299 with capital city, named as Söğüt. Eastern Roman Empire (Byzantine) goes out of existence in 1453, Anatolian Seljuk State goes out of existence in 1308 and Ottoman Empire goes out of existence in 1922. Republic of Turkey State was estabslished in Anatolia and Thrace territories since 1923. Now, let's see Turkey by beginning from Istanbul, which has become the capital city of three great emperorships, Roman, Byzantine and Ottoman:

Rumeli Fortress and Bosporus

ISTANBUL

It is shown in the excavations, performed in Yarımburgaz cave, located within boundaries of Küçükçekmece County that first settlements here go back to Paleolithic age. It is found in the excavations, performed in Fikirtepe and Pendik in Kadıköy in Anatolian side that settlement places go back to Chalcolithic period. Thracian origin Megarians came and settled in Sarayburnu under the leadership of Byzas in B.C. 667. They call their settled place here as Byzantium after their leader. City prospers and develops in a short time thanks to the marine trade. Byzantium and also Anatolia went under Persian soverenignty in B.C. Century VI. Byzantium participates into Attica-Delos union, established under the leadership of Athens in B.C. 478 in order to dispose of Persian soverenignty. After Alexander the Great demolished Persian Empire in B.C. 333, city enters into Macedonians' soverenignty. Romans went towards east in B.C. 2nd Century so city entered under the soverenignty of Roman Empire in B.C. 146. Byzantium was announced as new capital city of the emperorship by Roman Emperor Constantinus I (306-337) in A.D. 330 and city was called Constantinopolis. City was built to look like Roma with its large avenues, squares, monuments and beautiful structures. Even titles, such as "Second Roma" and "New Roma", are granted to such new city. After Roman Empire divides into two parts in 395, Constantinopolis survives as capital city in

Galata Bridge

Eastern Roman Empire. City witnesses the cruel robbery and ravage of Latins during Crusade IV. in 1204, emperorship losses its soverenignty. However, Eastern Roman (Byzantine) gains independence again in 1261. After Istanbul is conquered by Ottomans in 1453, Eastern Roman Empire goes out of existence. City becomes capital city of Ottoman State and survives under the name of Constantinopolis. Furthermore, Dersaadet, Darulhilafe, Deraliye and Asitane names are also used in the Ottoman period. After Ottoman State is collapsed, city losses its title of being capital city. It is named as Istanbul officially in 1925. Name of Istanbul is originated from "eis ten poli", which means "toward city" in Greek language.

Haydarpaşa

Yedikule Fortress

ISTANBUL WALLSAND YEDIKULE FORTRESS

City, located within the Historical Peninsula, is surrounded with extant walls, constructed during emperor II. Theodosios's (408-450) time. Walls, 21 km lenth, are composed of three parts as Land Walls, Sea of Marmara Walls and Golden Horn Walls. The walls in the direction of Golden Horn are destroyed completely; the walls in the direction of Sea of Marmara are standing partially. Land walls are preserved substantially. There are more than 50 gates and about 300 bastions on the walls. There are monumental gates such as Golden Gate (Porta Aurea), Belgrade Gate (Porta Xylokerko), Silivri Gate (Porta Selevria), Mevlana Gate (Myriandrion), Topkapi (Porta Hagios Romanos), Sulukule Gate (Porta Pempton), Edirne Gate (Porta Charsius) on the Land Walls. Yedikule Fortress is constructed adjacent to walls during the reign of Mehmed The Conqueror in 1470. State treasury and weapons are protected here in the first times. Afterwards, it is used as jailhouse. Sultan Osman II is killed here. Yedikule Fortress is open for visitation as monumental museum in these days.

Topkapı Palace, situated in the acropolis hill, which is known as the first establishment place of the city and seeing Istanbul Strait, Golden Horn, Sea of Marmara from a very scenic place, is in the position of citadel, bordered with walls, 5 km lenth, apart from the city along Hagia Sophia to Sarayburnu and is composed of four courtyards and Real Garden (Gülhane Park). Wall, surrounding Topkapı Palace, is called Sur-u Sultani and is constructed during the reign of Fatih and combined with Byzantine Walls in the coast. Topkapi Palace is constructed during the reign of Mehmed The Conqueror between 1472-1478 years. Palace is enlarged with outbuildings, built during the reign of subsequent sultans. It becomes center of state administration and residence of the sultans for a period of about four centuries. After Sultan Abdülmecit is moved to Dolmabahçe Palace, which he ordered to be constructed in Bosporus shores in 1856, Topkapı Palace is abandoned, however palace never losses its importance. It is the oldest and largest palace among the extant palac es due to its covered area in the worldwide. It is opened to public visits under the name of Topkapı Palace Mu seum in April 3, 1924 by the order of Ataturk. Topkapı Palace is entered through I. Courtyard, composed of four courtyards, through splendid Bab-i Hümayun (Imperial Gate) near Hagia Sophia. There are Saint Irene Church, which is open for public visits as monumental museum presently, Darphane-i Amire buildings and some storehouses and a small pavilion in the left in this field, which is called Alay Meydanı (I. Courtyard). There were buildings, constituting water treatment plants, belonging to the palace, called Gülhane Hospital, Has Fırını (Real Oven) and Dolap Ocağı (Cabinet Cooker) in the right of courtyard. II. Courtyard is entered through the monumental Babu-s Selam (Gate of Salutation) (Medial Gate) with two towers. This area, which is called Divan Square, is the ceremonial area, where the emperorship is managed and represented. There are Divan-ı Hümayun, called Kubbealtı with three domes and cloisters and Justice Tower on the left side. The treasury building with eight domes is situated adjacent to this building. Armor and weapons, used by Sultans and weapons of Ottoman, Memluk and Iran period, are exhibited in this building

A General View from Topkapı Palace

presently. Beşir Ağa Mosque and Hamam (Turkish Bath), Has Ahırlar (Real Barns), Zülüflü Baltacılar Koğuşu (Dorm) and Raht Hazine (Treasury) building are situated respectively in the lower area than Divan Square in the left. Palace Kitchens with twenty monumental chimneys extend thoroughly in the right side of II. Courtyard. Şekerciler Mosque is located in the farthest corner. Chinese and Japan ceramics, purchased or presented to the palace in Ottoman period, are exhibited in the palace kitchens presently. Turkish Kitchenware, Yıldız Porcelains and glass articles are exhibited in Helvahane and Şerbethane sections of the Kitchens. European porcelains and silvers are exhibited in the Dorm of Cooks building. III. Courtyard is also called "Harem-i Hümayun" (Imperial Harem) or "Enderun Meydanı (Enderun Square) and gate, which is entered from II. Courtyard, is called Babu-s Saade Gate (Akağalar Gate). It is the private courtyard of the Sultan (Padishah), nobody can enter from this gate without permission of Babu-s Saade Master. Accession, allegiance, greetings, foot council and funerals are used to be made in front of this gate, representing the Sultan. First structure in the entrance of III. Courtyard is Audience Chamber. Sultans are used to greet viziers, military judges, foreign ambassadors, guests here. III. Ahmet Library, constructed in 1719, is situated behind Audience Chamber. Chamber of Gate Master, Enderun School, Seferli Koğuşu (Imperial Wardrobe) building, in which caftans, and clothes belonging to sultan and dynasty, are exhibited, are located respectively in the right side of courtyard and building, called Fatih Pavilions / Enderun Treasury are situated in the corner. Treasury collection is exhibited in this section, composed of four rooms. The most famous exhibited works are Greeting-Accession, Evening Meal of Ramadan, Campaign and Rare Shah thrones, hanger and crests, which are Ottoman sultanate symbol, Topkapı dagger and spoon maker's diamond. The building, adjacent to Treasury building, is Kilerli Koğuşu, which is used as Museum management building presently. The building, located adjacent to it, is Hazine-i Hümayun (Imperial Treasury) Hademeler Koğuşu and Treasury of Weapons-master, in which various clocks are exhibited presently. The building, named as Has Oda (Sacred Chamber) (Hırka-i Saadet or Chamber of Sacred Relics) with four domes and constructed during the reign of Fatih, is situated in the left corner of courtyard. Sacred Chamber was the private residence of the sultans in their palace salutation place. Sultan is used to get into touch with mainly sultan's sons and also Enderun Masters and is used to greet divan viziers in this place, which is divided into sections such as Arzhane, Aslanhane and Has Oda. This place is used in order to exhibit Sacred Relics since Century XIX. Mohammed's sweater, swords, relics, Sancak-ı Şerif, swords of first caliphs and miscellaneous pieces of other celestial religions are exhibited there. Structure of Has Odalılar Dorm, in which portraits of sultans are exhibited, is situated next to this section. Ağalar Mosque, remaining from Fatih period in the direction of Harem in the courtyard, is used as the museum library at the present day. Akağalar Dorm and Kapıağası Hamam and tower are located in the left of Akağalar Gate. There is Revan Pavilion, built in memory of Revan Campaign of IV. Murat in 1639 on the marmoreal terrace

Inner Views from Topkapı Palace Museum

ion, built in memory of Bagdad Campaign of IV. Murat in 1639, Evening Meal of Ramadan Pergola, built by Sultan İbrahim in 1640, in IV. Courtyard of Topkapı Palace facing towards Sarayburnu. Structures such as Chamber of Chief Doctor, Mustafa Pasha Pavilion, Mecidiye Pavilion, built at the beginning of 1850, Dressing Room and Sofa Mosque, built in the neoclassical style in the middle of XIX. Century, are located in the garden of courtyard. IV. Courtyard is connected to Sacred Garden in the direction of Sarayburnu through a gate with two towers. Some pavilions, located in the coast, were destroyed during Sirkeci railway station and railway construction.

Hurrem Sultan starts to reside in Topkapı Palace as the first sultan wife, with her children. Structures, which are damaged due to a fire in Harem, are renewed in 1541. As Hürrem Sultan died in Old Palace in Beyazıt in 1558, Harem organization was not moved into Topkapı Palace yet. Some new structures are built in Harem during the reign of sultans, taking the lead after Fatih. After Sultan III. Murat becomes sultan in 1574, structures in Harem are repaired and sultan's harem is moved with its organization from Old Palace to Harem of Topkapı Palace, which is known as "New Palace". It is started to use the name of "Topkapı Palace" as of 1863. This name is

Harem-Topkapı Palace

HAREM

Mehmed The Conqueror has a palace for residence built in Bayezid Square after the conquest of Istanbul. As this palace becomes insufficient in the course of time, it has Topkapı Palace built between 1472-1478. First structures in Harem section are constructed in Fatih period. After the death of Hafsa sultan, who is the mother of Sultan Süleyman (Lawgiver) in 1534, passionate Haseki iven to the palace due to Topkapı, located in the coastal walls. The first structure, which is built in 1578-1579 in Harem, is the Chamber of III. Murat, which is the work of Sinan The Architect and known as Pavilion with Pool. Sultans, taking the lead after III. Murat, extend Harem area with built new structures and outbuildings.

Views from Hagia Sophia Museum

HAGIA SOPHIA MUSEUM

Hagia Sophia, which is used as museum at the present, was constructed in such a short period of five years between 532-537 and during the period of Eastern Roman Emperor I. Iustinianos (527-565). Architects of Hagia Sophia Church are Anthemios from Tralles (Aydın) and Isidoros from Miletus (Balat-Söke). Church has a basilical plan. It is composed of galleries, with abscissa, three naves, two narthexes as inside and outside one, which surround the structure inwardly from three directions and are stepped up through ramps from four corners of the structure. Structure is in the internal sizes of 100 x 70 m. Dome is in the average diameter of 31,5 m. and its height from the ground is 55 m. There are 40 windows in tambour of the dome. 40 columns are used in the ground floor of the structure and 67 columns are used in the galleries and total used columns are 107 pieces. Internal walls of the structure are covered with marmoreal sheets with various colors. Again top sections of internal walls and dome and vault covers are coated with mosaics. Some of mosaics are fallen out. All of mosaics with figures belong to the period after 9th Century. There are Vestibule Mosaic, depicting The Virgin Mary, Jesus The Child, Emperor Constantine I. (306-337) and Iustinianos I, in the south gate of the structure; Imperial Mosaic, depict ing Emperor VI. Leon (886-912), The Virgin Mary and The Archangel Gabriel, on the middle door, opened from Internal narthex to main location and called "Emperor Gate"; Mosaic of The Virgin Mary and Jesus The Child in her lap in the abscissa and The Archangel Gabriel in Bema vault in the right; Deisis mosaic, depicting The Virgin Mary, Jesus and John the Baptist (Yahya) in the south gallery wall; mosaic images of Emperor Constantine Monomakhos (1042-1055) and Empress Zoe in the left and Emperor Ioannes Komnenos (1118-1143), Empress Eirene and their child Alexios in the right in east wall of south gallery. There are mosaic of Emperor Alexandros (912-913) in the internal wall of north gallery; mosaic descriptions of saints named as Ioannes Khyrisostomos, Young Ignatios and Ignatios Theophoros in niches in the internal front of north wall of the structure. Hagia Sophia is converted into mosque after conquest of Istanbul in 1453. A great restoration is conducted between 1847-1849 during the reign of Sultan Abdülmecit (1839-1861). Structure is converted into museum

Views from Hagia Sophia Museum

in November 24, 1934 and it is opened for public visits as museum in 1935. Four minarets are added from outside to the structure and niche, pulpit, muezzin and Sultan messes, preach desk are added into it in the Ottoman period; tables, containing names of Allah, Mohammad, first four caliphs (Abu Bakr, Umar, Uthman, Ali) and grandsons of Mohammad, named as Hassan and Hussein, are hung in its internal walls. The Light Surah is written onto the main dome. Library structure is added among buttresses in south direction of the structure. There are structures of Baptism place, Muvakkithane (time adjusting house), Ottoman Elementary-Primary School, Water-Tank With a Fountain, School remains, Almshouse and Chamber of Treasury and also burial place, containing Sultan II. Selim (1566-1574), III. Murat (1574-1595), III. Mehmet (1595-1603) and Tomb of Sultan's Sons, Sultan I. Mustafa (1617-1623) and Sultan İbrahim (1640-1648), in the garden of museum. Sultan Pavilion, which is used as small mosque at the present, is located in Topkapı Palace direction of Hagia Sophia.

Blue Mosque (Back Page)

Blue Mosque

SULTAN AHMET MOSQUE (BLUE MOSQUE) AND SOCIAL COMPLEX

Sultan Ahmet Mosque is constructed by chief architect Sedefkar Mehmet Ağa during the reign of Ottoman sultan I. Ahmet (1603-1617) and it is started to construct Sultan Ahmet Mosque in 1609 and construction of mosque is completed in 1617, however, construction of other structures in the social complex lasts until 1620. Therefore, Sultan I. Ahmet, died after opening of mosque in 1617, could be buried into his tomb, which is constructed during the reign of his son II. Osman in 1620. Sultan Ahmet Mosque is the most splendid and magnificent work of Ottoman architecture after the classical period. Mosque is surrounded with a large outer courtyard, which is entered from eight gates, of which three ones are from the front. Inner courtyard of the mosque, entered from three gates, is surrounded with 26 columns and 30 cloisters with domes and there is an octagonal water-tank with a fountain with column and dome in the middle of the courtyard. Mosque has six minarets and there are three minaret balconies in each of four minarets in external environment of the main space and there are two minaret balconies in each of two minarets in the courtyard edges. Inner space of the mosque is in the sizes of 64m x 72m. Dome, covering main space of the mosque, is in the height of 43 m and in the diameter of 23,5 m and it is placed on four main archways based on four elephant feet. Main dome is supported with four semi-domes. There are messes in two sides and on the top of main entrance. Sultan Mess is located in the left corner and Çilehane of sultan is located near it. Furthermore, structure of Imperial Pavilion, constructed independently from the mosque, is located here. Niche and pulpit within the mosque is decorated and made from marble. Mosque has 260 windows with round archway. Inner walls of the mosque is covered with tile boards, dated back to end of XVI. Century and beginning of XVII. Century, until the cornices. 21043 tiles are used in these decorations. Main dome, semi-domes and archways are decorated with the hand-drawn works. Mosque is also called "Blue Mosque" due to this tile and hand-drawn decorations. Pearl and tortoise shell workmanship of mosque's gate and windows, are made by the architect of mosque Sedefkar Mehmet Ağa. Handwritings in the mosque belong to Ahmet Gubari, who is the famous calligraphist of that period. Structures of social complex are stood in line around the mosque. There are School, Muvakkithane, Koran Reading Chamber, called Dar-ul Kurra, Public Fountain with courtyard with four directions, which are surrounded with cloisters and two floors, constructed in the north direction and outside the outer courtyard of the mosque; shops, Ottoman Elementary-Primary School, Sultan I. Ahmet's Tomb and other religious and educational structures in the direction of Horse Square (Hippodrome). There is Sultan Pavilion, located in the outer courtyard in the north direction of the mosque and used as Carpet Museum by General Directorate of Foundations at the present. There are Ottoman Bazaar (Bazaar) and Turkish bath, extending in parallel with the mosque in kiblah side of the mosque. Public Soup-Kitchen and Hospital, belonging to social complex, located on the cliff round terrace (spendone) in the sea side of Hippodrome, are demolished considerably. sizes of 120 x 400m. was in the form of rectangular, extending in the direction of northern east and southern west and its southern west edge finished in the form of semicircle edge, called sphendone. Entrance part of Hippodrome was in the direction of Hagia Sophia Square. Emperors are used to watch ceremonies, cart races, festivals, plays in the Hippodrome from their loggias in Katisma Palace, having connection with Hippodrome and located in the place, where Sultan Ahmet Mosque is situated. Hippodrome is used to witness social meetings, political conflicts in the Roman and Byzantine periods. Conflicts are used to be especially between Greens and Blues, who are two opposite

Blue Mosque Inside

Dikilitaş (Hippodrome) Back Page

HIPPODROME / SULTANAHMET SQUARE / HORSE SQUARE

Hippodrome / Sultanahmet Square / Horse Square: Horse Square is the name, which is given to the area in front of Sultan Ahmet Mosque by Ottomans until XIX. Century. As it is known, there was a Hippodrome structure in Byzantine period here and horse cart races are used to be organized here. Hippodrome, which is started to be constructed by Roman Emperor Septimius Severus (193-211), could be completed in 325 during the period of emperor Constantine The Great I (306-337). Structure in the

groups. Hippodrome suffers great damage as well as many structures during Nika Riot, occurred in Hippodrome in 532. Horse Square also witnesses triumphal processions, glorious weddings, meetings, festivals, plays, important historical and social events in the Ottoman period. Monuments such as Obelisk, Wreathed Column, Brick Column were located on the wall with large partition, called spina in the height of human, with open edges and dividing Hippodrome Square into two parts from the middle and thoroughly.

OBELISK

It is the obelisk, which is placed in front of Carnac Temple, in order to monumentalize Egyptian pharaoh III. Tutmosis' passage beyond Euphrates River in B.C. 1471. Obelisk is pink granite and single piece and four-cornered and there are hieroglyph scripts on it. Such obelisk, which is brought from Egypt to Constantinopolis in the period of emperor Grand Theodosios (378-395), is placed into its place in the Hippodrome in 390.

GERMAN FOUNTAIN

Fountain, located in Horse Square (Hippodrome), which is made by architect Spitta and Carlitzik and Italian architect Joseph Antony in 1899-1901 by the order of German Emperor II. Wilhelm in honor of 15th sultanate anniversary of Sultan II. Abdülhamit's acceding to the throne, is brought to Istanbul and assembled into its place. Fountain is a structure, which is mixture of German renaissance, Byzantine and Ottoman water-tanks with a fountain with ophite columns on marmoreal octagonal base and round archways among them and with its copper covered dome. Dome is covered with golden mosaic from inside and initials and signatures of Emperor and Sultan are engraved.

German Fountain

BRICK COLUMN

It is the obelisk, bricked with grinded stones. This Brick Column was covered with bronze sheets in its time. Probably, Brick Column, which was supposed to be constructed in the period of emperor Constantine The Great, was repaired in the period of emperor Constantinus VII Porphyrogennetos (913-959). While city was plundered during IV. Crusade in 1204, bronze sheets of the column was destroyed.

Basilica Cistern - Medusa

WREATHED COLUMN

Wreathed Column, which is casted by melting bronze booties, which are obtained by Greeks from Persians, whom they beat in Salamis and Platea battles in B.C. 479, is presented to Temple of Apollo in Delphi Island. Column is composed of three intertwined serpents. There is a golden trivet on three serpent heads, separated from each other on the top, and a golden vessel in the diameter of about three meters on this trivet. When Emperor Grand Constantinius (306-337) has this column carried from Delphi Island to here in 330, trivet and vessel on Wreathed Column are absent.

BASILICA CISTERN

Cistern is built in 527 by Emperor Iustinianos I (527-565) and constructed in order to convey water for Hagia Sophia and Emperorship Palace. Cistern is named after basilica, which is located here in advance and in the position of cultural center. Furthermore, it is also known as Iustinianos Cistern. When Turks, who come to Anatolia firstly, encounter with a cistern, take it for an underground column forest for the first time, they call here as Yerebatan Cistern because they likened this place to a palace, going down the ground. Cistern is used to be fed by water, carried by Valens (Bozdoğan) aqueducts. Basilica Cistern is the single cistern, maintaining its function in Istanbul up to the close periods. So, it provided water even for Topkapı Palace gardens. Basilica Cistern is in the form of rectangle and in the sizes of 65 x 138 m. There are 336 columns (12 x 28), carrying cross vaults with 8 meters ground clearance in the cistern. It is seen that two mythological marmoreal Medusa's heads, of which one is side and the other is upside down, are put under two short columns in the cistern. After restoration and clean-

Turkish and Islamic Works Museum

ing work is made within the cistern by Istanbul Metropolitan Municipality between 1985-1987, walkways are built into the cistern and it is opened for public visit.

MILION STONE

There was Augustinian Square, surrounded with colonnaded cloisters in front of Hagia Sophia Church in Byzantine Age. Monumental Milion Stone (Milestone) is erected in the beginning point no: 0 (zero) of Mesė Avenue (Divanyolu) in the center of Istanbul and of the road, named as Triumph Way of Byzantine", and going from Istanbul to Rome in Basilica Cistern side of this square. Top of this stone was decorated with sculptures and reliefs in its time. It is widely told first erected milestone is "Golden Milion Stone". There are remains of water gauge, belonging to Ottoman period and increasing like a tower and adjusting water pressure and damaged considerably, immediately near this stone.

TURKISH AND ISLAMIC ARTS MUSEUM

Museum, which is opened for public visits under the name of Islamic Foundations Museum in 1914 in Almshouse building, located within Süleymaniye Social Complex, which is the opus of Sinan the Architect, is the first Turkish museum, where Turkish and Islamic Arts are exhibited collectively. Museum is called Turkish and Islamic Arts Museum in the period after Republic. Museum is moved into Ibrahim Pasha Palace in 1983. Ibrahim Pasha Palace, located just opposite Sultan Ahmet Mosque, was constructed on the northern-west space of Hippodrome. The remains of Hippodrome were also used during the construction. Sultan and people around him used to watch the festivals, march parades in Horse Square, in the loggia and balcony of Ibrahim Pasha Palace. Palace is one of the most important Ottoman civil architectural models of XVI. century and it is given as a gift to grand vizier Ibrahim Pasha by Suleyman The Magnificent in 1520. After the death of Ibrahim Pasha in 1536, palace is used in the services such as barracks, sewing workshop, janissary band house, jail. Section, which is used as museum at the present time, is great ceremony saloon and its surrounding section and 2nd courtyard of the palace. Excellent arts of all periods of Islamic art are exhibited in the museum. tions in the museum. Some of them are Siyer-i Nebi of famous calligraphist Ahmet Karahisari, explaining Koran and Life of Prophets, and work, named as Zübde-tüt Tevarih with miniature, recording Turkish and Islamic history until the reign of Sultan III. Murat, Koran case covers with the pearl inlay and reading desks, 1251 dated wooden sarcophagus of Seyyit Mahmut Hayrani and also excellent models of metal, glass, tile and calligraphy arts. Furthermore, museum has also the ethnographic arts section. Carpet and rug looms, woven pieces, wool dying techniques, carpet weaving and embroidery art models, collected from various regions of Anatolia, cos

Big Palace Mosaics Museum

Art works, which are exhibited in the museum, are composed of Carpet Art collection, Wooden Art Collection, Manuscripts and Calligraphy collection, Stone Arts collection, Metal Arts collection, Ceramic and Glass Art collections. The wealthiest one of these collections is the Carpet collection, containing the most beautiful models of Seljuk and Ottoman period. The most beautiful models of carpet, prayer rug and rug of Uşak, Gördes, Bergama, Ladik, Milas, Sivas, Konya, Kars, are exhibited. It is possible to see extremely unique arts of other collec- tumes are exhibited in its local richness and house wares, handicrafts, handicraft equipments, migratory tents are exhibited in its peculiar locations here.

GRAND PALACE / GRAND PALACE MOSAIC MUSEUM

The area, beginning from Hippodrome and Hagia Sophia, extending to Sea of Marmara, is the region of Palaces. We learn details about Byzantine palaces from the extant written documents of historians and historiographers of that period. The most comprehensive of these is “Ceremonies” or “Book of Ceremony,” famous work of emperor VII. Constantine Porphyrogennetos (944-959). Researchers apply to this work for reference of names, unknown places, inner equipments, positions of Byzantine Palaces. Also we learn details about Grand Palace and other Byzantine palaces from memoirs of Italian ambassador Liutprand, who visits Constantinopolis in 9th Century and “Aleksios” named work of Anna Komnena, who is the daughter of emperor Alexios (1081-1118). It was entered into Grand Palace, spreading into a large space in southern east direction of Sultan Ahmet Mosque and Hagia Sophia from the gate, named as Bronze Gate (Chalke) in Augustinian Square, surrounded with cloisters and located in front of Hagia Sophia Church. Structures such as palaces, palace guardian barracks, luxurious pictorial structures, churches, libraries, meeting buildings, luxurious palace residences, ceremony saloons are constructed in the space, arranged in the form of terraces. Grand Palace, which is built during the period of Constantine The Great, suffers great damage during Nika Riot in 532 and emperor Iustinianos I (527-565) gets the structure repaired. Emperors, taking the lead, make new structures and extend the space. Emperors abandon such great palaces with excessive costs, at the beginning of 10th century and reside in the smaller palaces such as Magnaura and Blakherna. Grand Palace, which is plundered during the Crusade in 1204, is abandoned in the last periods of Byzantine. A small Turkish district is constituted in this space after the conquest of Istanbul in 1453 by Ottomans. As remains of destroyed structures and soils, arisen from foundation excavations are thrown into Area of Palaces especially during construction of Sultan Ahmet Mosque and Social

Istanbul Archeology Museum

Complex in this area in the Ottoman period, all structure remains of Byzantine period are underground for meters. Floor mosaics of Grand Palace are unearthed at the end of excavations from underground for meters, of Sultanahmet Bazaar, which is constructed here. A courtyard with peristillium and having a floor, covered with mosaics and surrounded with columns of Grand Palace, is unearthed as a result of excavations of English scientists around Bazaar within Sultan Ahmet Mosque Social Complex between 1935-1938 and monster Khimaera, the child feeding his donkey, fight between elephant and lion. Colored stone, color ed glass and earthenware mosaic pieces are used as material. As they are the floor mosaics, religious symbols and motifs, which are used in the Christian art, are not used. Museum is opened for public visits in 1953. Restoration and conservation works of mosaics are performed and completed between 1983-1997 years within the cooperation between Republic of Turkey Ministry of Culture and Austrian Academy of Sciences.

A View from Istanbul Archeology Museum

ISTANBUL - ARCHAEOLOGY MUSEUMS

and 1951-1954. Floor mosaics cover an area with 250 square meters. Scenes from nature, human life and mythology are depicted in these mosaics, dated as first half of A.D. 6th century. Some of depicted scenes are tiger hunting, mask with acanthus beard, gazelle grassing, fight between eagle and snake, shepherds herding goose, children at camel's back, man milking the goat, bear eating the lamb, mare sucking her colt, wood load ed mule pulling down the rider at its back, Bellerophon

Istanbul Archaeology Museums, located on Osman Hamdi Bey ramp, rising to Topkapı Palace Museum from the right of entrance of Gülhane Park, are composed of three museums as Archaeology Museum, Old Eastern Arts Museum and Enameled Kiosk Museum. It is one of the biggest museums of the world. It accommodates more than one million arts. Museum collections have the arts, including cultural values of various civilizations, containing a large geography from Balkans, Anatolia, Syria, Palestine, Arabian Peninsula, Egypt, Iraq to Afghanistan.

A) ARCHAEOLOGY MUSEUM

Museum is composed of two structures as Main building (Old structure) and Outbuilding (New structure). Architect Aleksandre Vallaury constructs main building by the order of Mr. Osman Hamdi at the end of 19th Century, and construction of Imperial Museum is completed in 1891, 1902 and 1908 in three stages. Section, where Sayda sarcophaguses are located, is opened for public visits under the name of "Museum of Sarcophaguses" in June 13, 1891. This structure is the first Turkish museum. Building has two floors and its exterior front is made by being inspired from Crying Women Sarcophagus. It is one of the most beautiful models of neoclassical structures in Istanbul. Alexander Sarcophagus, Crying Women Sarcophagus, Satrap Sarcophagus, Lycia Sarcophagus, Tabnit Sarcophagus, situated in Sayda King Tombs; Sidamara Sarcophagus, Erosus Sarcophagus, brought from other ancient cities and regions and other Sarcophaguses and also architectural elements, sculpture and reliefs, tombstones, altars, mosaics, belonging to various temples are exhibited in a chronological order from archaic age to the end of Byzantine period in the ground floor of the main building. Some of important arts are Head of Alexander the Great, Marsyas, Goddess Tykhe, Nymphe, Ephebos sculptures and busts of emperor Marcus Aurelius and empress Faustina. Small sized stone pieces, pots and pans, earthenware statuettes are exhibited in the second floor. Also there are treasury department and Non Islamic and Islamic coin cabinets, containing approximately 800 000 coins, stamps, signs, medals, and coin casts; and a rich library, including about 70 000 books in this floor. Outbuilding is adjacent to southern-east of main building. It is composed of six floors. There are old art depots in the second floor under the ground. Kid's Museum is located in the ground floor and also some architectural structures are exhibited here. Thrace, Bithinia, Byzantine (Surrounding Cultures of Istanbul) works are exhibited under this ground floor. Works of Istanbul For Ages are exhibited in 1st floor, works of Anatolia and Troia For Ages are exhibited in 2nd floor and works, containing various periods belonging to Anatolia and Surrounding Cultures (Cyprus, Syria, Palestine) are exhibited in 3rd floor.

B) OLD EASTERN ARTS MUSEUM

Mr. Osman Hamdi gets Sanayi-i Nefise Mekteb-i (Fine Arts Academy) constructed in 1883 and the structure has two floors. It is arranged as museum between 1917-1919 and 1932-1935 years. Museum is closed for public visits in 1963 and its internal locations are modernized and it is opened for public visits again in 1974. Arabian Works Before Islam, Egypt Works, Mesopotamia Works, Anatolian Works are exhibited in the top floors of the

Istanbul Tile Museum

museum. Tablet of Kadesh Peace and Friendship Agreement, which is made between Hittites and Egyptians in B.C. 1269 and is the first "peace and friendship" agreement in the history, is present in this museum. There is a rich "tablet archive", composed of about 75 000 tablets with cuneiform script in the museum. Ground floor of the museum is used as old art depot and office.

A View from Grand Bazaar

C) ENAMELED KIOSK MUSEUM

Mehmed The Conqueror gets Enameled Kiosk building, which is one of the oldest civil architecture models in Istanbul, constructed in 1472. It is used as Müze-i Hümayun (Imperial Museum) between 1875-1891 years. It is opened for public visits under the name of Fatih Museum, in which Turkish and Islamic Arts are exhibited in 1953 due to 500th anniversary of Istanbul conquest. It is transferred to Istanbul - Archaeology Museums in 1981. Entrance front of kiosk, which is constructed in a sloped land, is constructed with single floor and its back front is constructed with two floors. There is a marmoreal cloister, composed of 14 columns in the entrance. It is entered into the kiosk from shed shaped portal, covered with mosaic tiles. Inner location of kiosk is composed of middle saloon and six lateral rooms. Various tile and ceramic works of Seljuk and Ottoman periods are exhibited in the kiosk. Tile oil-lamp and blue-white tile plates, made in İznik, are among the most valuable works of the museum. Furthermore, Kütahya and Çanakkale ceramics constitute the significant part of the tile collection in the museum. There are approximately 2000 works in the saloons and depots of Enameled Kiosk Museum.

GRAND BAZAAR

The place, where Grand Bazaar is located, was in the position of trade center in Byzantine period. Mehmed The Conqueror get Covered Bazaar and Sandal Bazaar constructed between 1455-1461 in order to enrich the economic life in the city, which he makes capital city after conquest of Istanbul. Then, Grand Bazaar is constituted with shops and hostelries, which are constructed around these bazaars. There are 24 hostelries, 440 shops and 65 streets within the bazaar. Furthermore, bazaar has 18 gates, of which 8 gates are big and 10 gates are small. Bazaar has witnessed many fires and earthquakes and undergone many repairs up to now.

Süleymaniye Mosque - Süleymaniye Mosque Inside

SULEYMANIYE MOSQUE AND SOCIAL COMPLEX

It is constructed between 1550-1557 by Sinan The Architect by the order of Süleyman The Magnificent. Mosque is the semiskilled period of Sinan The Architect. It is entered into outer courtyard of the mosque from 10 gates. Inner courtyard is in the form of rectangle and it has three gates, of which one is in the center and others are in the sides. Inner courtyard is surrounded with cloisters with domes, carried by the columns. There is a rectangular water tank with a fountain in the middle of courtyard. Mosque has four minarets and its two minarets have three minaret balconies and the other two minarets have two minaret balconies. It is entered into the mosque from three gates, of which one is from the front and the others are from the sides. Mosque has a plan, which is close to square, and it is in the sizes of 69 x 68m. Main dome is 53 m ground clearance and diameter of the dome is 26,5m. Main dome is placed on four main archways based on four elephant feet. There is one semi dome on each of niche and entrance gate. Four columns are also placed between elephant feet in two sides within the mosque. Thus, inner space is enlarged with five domes, which are placed to each of archways, connected to these columns and much more

community enables praying. There are 138 windows in the mosque. There are boards, composed of 16th Century İznik tiles in two sides of niche. Pulpit, niche, muezzin and Sultan Messes within the mosque are marmoreal and reflect the magnificent models of the workmanship. Dome has hand-drawn decorations. Scripts within the mosque belong to Ahmet Karahisari and Hasan Çelebi. There are structures, composed of Evvel Madrasah (theological school), Sani Madrasah, School of Medicine, Rabi Madrasah, Salis Madrasah, Tabhane, Daruzziyafe, Bimarhane, Darulhadis Madrasah, Hamam, Darul Kurra, Tomb of Süleyman The Magnificent, Tomb of Hürrem Sultan (Roxelane), Chamber of Tomb Guardian and Tomb of Sinan The Architect other than the mosque within Süleymaniye Social Complex. Evvel Madrasah and Sani Madrasah are used as Süleymaniye Library at the present time.

Kariye Museum

KARIYE (CARIA) MUSEUM / CHORA MONASTERY CHURCH

Caria, situated in Edirnekapı district within Istanbul walls, is derived from "Chora", which means outside the city or rural area in ancient Greek language. Although its construction date is not known certainly, it is known that there is a chapel here previously. Caria Church is also constructed with the monastery in 536 during the period of Emperor Iustinianos I. (527-565). The church is destroyed in the iconization period (724-843), and it is repaired in various periods. Moving imperial dynasty into Blahernai Palace in Comnenuses Periods (1081-1185), organization of some rituals in Caria Church, which is close to the palace, increases the importance of the church. Consequently, Maria Doukania, who is mother-in-law of emperor I. Alexios (1081-1118), takes the church under her protection and gets ruined church restored. Church is plundered and witnesses a great destruction during Latin Invasion (1204-1261). Church has its prime period during the reign of emperor Andronikos II. Palaiologos (1282-1328). Theodoros Metokhides, who is the great government man, politician, man of letters and scholar in that period, gets the church repaired substantially. A vestibule is added into north wing of the church, composed of narthex and main space; Parekklesion, which is a narrow and long chapel with single nave next to south front and external narthex, extending along the west front. Furthermore, mosaics, decorating internal and external narthex, and frescoes, decorating the parekklesion, are made in this period. The richest mosaic and frescoes of last golden age of Byzantine are present in Caria. Life of The Virgin Mary and Jesus are illustrated in the mosaics, decorating wall, archway, vault and domes in the internal and external narthex. The life history of The Virgin Mary are illustrated in the north wing of internal narthex and important events of The Holy Family, birth and baptism of Jesus are illustrated in the north wing of external narthex. Miracles and performed affairs of Jesus are located in south wings of both narthexes. Some subjects of Old Testament, which are considered as very important by Christianity, are depicted in the frescoes, decorating Parekklesion. Scene of Death of The Virgin Mary (Koimesis), located on the gate in the main space, affects the audience particularly. Scenes of Resurrection (Anastasis) and The Last Judgment (Deesis) attract attention with their sizes in Parekklesion. Scene of Resurrection (Anastasis) is the inarguable masterpiece of Christian picture art with its magnificence and picturesque. Furthermore, niches, located in inner walls of internal and external narthexes and Parekklesion, are used as grave for famous people.

FETHIYE MUSEUM / PAMMAKARISTOS MONASTERY CHURCH

Pammakaristos Monastery Church, located in Fatih County Çarşamba quarter, is constructed on behalf of The Virgin Mary, by Mihail Glabas Tarkaniotes, who is one of the prominent chara r the narthex, main space is covered with a drummed dome with 12 windows. Its main dome has 12 slices and mosaic image of Jesus is located in its middle section and mosaic images of the prophets in Old Testament are located in the slices. There are mosaic depictures, containing scene of Deesis (judgment day), composed of Jesus, The Virgin Mary and Ioannes in the abscissa section. Furthermore, there are mosaics and frescoes, containing Saint

Fethiye Museum

After Istanbul is conquered in 1453 by Turks, Caria Church maintains its function for a period more. However, church is turned into the mosque by Hadım Ali Pasha, who is grand vizier of Sultan II. Bayezit (1481-1512) in 1511. A minaret is added into south edge of external narthex. It is not touched to the mosaics and frescoes. Only they are covered with plaster and wooden shutters. Caria is turned into the museum in 1945. Structure undergoes a great repair between 1948-1958 and all mosaics and frescoes are cleaned and brought out into the open.

depictures in the archways and vaults. The structure is used as women's monastery after conquest of Istanbul and used as Rum Patriarchate for 150 years of 1455. It is turned into the mosque by Ahmet Pasha at the end of 16th Century (1590) and it is called "Fethiye Mosque" in memory of conquest of Azerbaijan and Georgia. Mosque is damaged in the fire of Balatkapı in 1640. Mosque undergoes repair in 1845 according the epigraph, located on the south gate of the mosque. Mosque, undergoing a great repair between

1936-1938 years, is opened for praying just in 1960s. Parekklesion, which is the grave chapel of the church, is repaired in the same years, all mosaics and frescoes inside it are brought out into the open by American Byzantine Institute. Section of Parekklesion is open for public visits under the name of "Fethiye Museum" at the present time.

GOLDEN HORN (HALİÇ)

According to a Greek legend, Io disguised as cow, passing Bosporus (Istanbul Strait), hides herself in a sheltered place of Keras (current name: Haliç) and gives birth to her daughter Keroessa there. As you see, Keras (horn in Greek), name of Haliç, is derived from Keroessa. Then, Keroessa is married to god of seas, Poseidon and their child, Byzas establishes city of Istanbul. Haliç, which is called Golden horn by Westerns, starts from Sarayburnu and in the other side, Galata and extend to the place, where Kağıthane and Alibeyköyü streams flow into the sea. New Galata Bridge, Unkapanı Bridge and Ataturk Bridges, connecting two sides to each other, are situated on Haliç. Old Galata Bridge is also protected on Haliç. Haliç was the natural harbor of the city. There were factories, workshops, shipyards on its two sides for the convenience of marine transportation previously. Most of them were eliminated in the last thirty years and surrounding of Halic was opened. Now, let's try to know historical structures around Haliç by starting from the side of historical peninsu la.Sepetçiler Pavilion, located on the shore between Sarayburnu and Sirkeci Railway Station, is constructed by the order of Sultan Ibrahim on the place of an old kiosk, which is destroyed in 1643, in order to enable harem peoples to watch marine festivals. Kiosk, which is renewed during the reign of I. Mahmut, serves as International Press Centre at the present time.

RUSTEM PASHA MOSQUE

Mosque, which is located in Eminonu district and is a part of Rustem Pasha Social Complex, is constructed by Sinan The Architect in 1560. Inner space and last prayer place of the mosque are covered with 16th Century İznik tiles thoroughly and mosque appears almost as a tile museum. There are 41 different tulip ornament images on the tiles.

NEW MOSQUE

Safiye Sultan, mother of Sultan III. Murat, initiates the construction of mosque in Eminönü in 1597. Architect of the mosque is Davut Ağa. After death of Davut Ağa, works are maintained by Dalgıç Ahmet Ağa. Construction of the mosque is ceased upon death of Safiye Sultan in 1603. Construction of mosque can be completed by Head of Architect Mustafa Ağa, by the order of Hatice Sultan, mother of Sultan IV. Mehmet in 1664. Inner space and last prayer place of the mosque are covered with tiles thoroughly. New Mosque and Social Complex is the last model of classical Ottoman architecture style. Spice Bazaar and tomb of Turhan Sultan are located within the structure group, constructed as Social complex.

Rüstempaşa Mosque Inside

FATIH MOSQUE

Mosque, located in Fatih district, is situated within the social complex, which is constructed between 1467-1470 by the order of Mehmed The Conqueror for his own name. Architect of the mosque is Atik Sinan. Mosque is ruined substantially in the earthquake in 1765 and Sultan III.Mustafa gets the mosque repaired by architect Mehmet Tahir Ağa. There are architectural structures, composed of 16 madrasahs, soup kitchen, hostel, old Turkish hospital, library, muvakkithane (time adjusting house), hamam, Ottoman elementary-primary school and two tombs within the social complex other

Süleymaniye Mosque

than the mosque. It is possible to see many mosques, churches and synagogues and civil architecture models in Cibali, Fener, Balat and Ayvansaray districts. Furthermore, Center of Orthodox Rum Patriarchate is also situated in Fener. Anemas dungeons and extant and standing Feudal Landlord's Palace from Byzantine period, are the important structures, which are required to be visited. Building of Fez Factory, constructed for production of fez during the reign of II. Mahmut in 1835, is located in Defterdar district in the right side of Ataturk Bridge.

EYUP SULTAN MOSQUE AND TOMB

Mosque is located in Eyup district, and mosque and a tomb are constructed in the place where Eyyub El-Ensari, who is martyr during blockade of Istanbul by Arabians in 669, is burie d, by the order of Mehmed The Conqueror after the conquest of Istanbul in 1458. Mosque is destroyed dur ing the reign of Sultan III. Selim and extant and current mosque is constructed between 1789-1800. Eyüp Sultan Tomb is repaired repeatedly and outbuildings are constructed until it reaches today from Ottoman period. It is embellished with the most beautiful tile boards of İznik and Kütahya. Eyüp Sultan Tomb gains great importance because it is the location, where putting on sword ceremony of Ottoman Sultans is organized. Here is turned into a sacred place since establishment of Eyüp Sultan Mosque and tomb. This case attracts attention of Western travelers. Pierre Loti is one of the western travelers, who are interested in the oriental mysticism. The place where Pierre Loti sits and watches the sunset is called "Pierre Loti Cafe" or "Pierre Loti Hill" nowadays. Eyüp is a district of tombs at the same time. There are tombs of Mihrisah Valide Sultan, mother of III.Selim, Sokollu Mehmet Pasha and Husrev Pasha and many people at degree of government man in Ottoman period here other than Eyüp Sultan tomb. We can tell the following things by beginning from Galata in the opposite shore of Haliç. Beyoğlu, which is called Pera by Westerns, is modern European side of Ottoman in 19th

Century. There were foreign country embassies, churches and quarters in Beyoğlu and there were business places of foreign businessmen, merchants, bankers in Galata.

GALATA TOWER

Tower is constructed as the main tower of Galata Walls by Genoeses in 1348. Tower, which is damaged substantially due to earthquake in 1509, is repaired again. It is used as dungeon and fire tower in the miscellaneous periods. Tower with cylindrical body and covered with conical roof is in the height of 68 m and has 12 floors.

MUSEUM OF DIVAN LITERATURE

Structure, which is located in Tunel district and used of Mevlevi Lodge, is constructed instead of Mevlevi Lodge, which is burned during the reign of III. Mustafa in 1766. Mevlevi Lodge, which is constructed in the form of Social Complex is composed of semahane, dervishes' cells, sheikh chamber and sultan mess, women's section, library, public fountain, muvakkithane (time adjusting house), kitchen, tombs and graveyard. It is turned into a museum, in which divans of Divan poets, manuscripts, musical instruments and mevlevi objects are exhibited, in 1975.

AYNALIKAVAK PAVILION

It is situated within a large garden behind Haliç Shipyard. It is constructed during the reign of Sultan III Ahmet (1703-1730). It is turned into the pavilion lastly during the reign of Sultan III. Selim (1789-1807). Sultan III. Selim makes his compositions here. Pavilion is arranged as Museum Of Classical Turkish Musical Instruments.

RAHMI KOC MUSEUM

Museum, which is located in Hasköy and opened for public visits in 2001, exhibits the vehicles, reflecting development history of land, air, railway and marine transportation and extant industrial and engineering works, belonging to various periods.

Galata Tower

Maiden Tower

MINIATURK

Miniature models of various historical buildings and sites, located in Anatolian territories, are exhibited in this area, which is bound to Istanbul Metropolitan Municipality and opened for public visits in 2003.

THE BOSPORUS

According to myth, Byzas was the son of Keroessa, who is daughter of god of seas Poseidon and head god Zeus and he was born in a place, close to this city. Name of current Haliç was Keroessa. Byzas surrounded the city, which he established with assistances of god Apollo and Poseidon, with walls. Bosporus, which is the name of Istanbul Strait, is used with the meaning of "Cow passage", "Ox passage" or "Calf passage". It has its own myth as follows: According to myth, god of the gods Zeus falls in love with Io, who is daughter of Argos king. As Io also falls in love with Zeus, Io becomes pregnant. However, Zeus is afraid of evil action of his wife Hera and disguises his lover as cow and hides her. Hera is aware of the case and she causes cow disguised Io bother with the horse fly. As horse fly disturbs the cow, cow can not grass and escapes continuously. While cow is escaping from place to place continuously, it passes from Istanbul Strait. Therefore, Istanbul Strait is called Bosporus.

MAIDEN'S TOWER

Maiden's Tower is constructed on a rocky place, in the shore of Harem and Salacak in the side of Istanbul Strait, which opens to Sea of Marmara and serves as lighthouse. Its height is 18 m. Tower undergoes a great repair in the recent periods. It provides service for touristic purpose at the present time. Athenian commander Alkibiyades constructs a control tower, made of stone, on the rocks over the sea in the shores of Salacak in order to keep battleships and merchant ships, passing from Black Sea to Sea of Marmara under control and to observe them. Such control and observation tower is extended at the period of Eastern Roman Empire, during the reign of emperor Manuel I. Comnenos (1143-1180) and is turned into a square plan. After Istanbul is conquered by Ottomans in 1453, tower serves as the lighthouse. After tower is ruined as a result of a fire, it is constructed from stone again during the reign of III. Ahmet (1703-1730). Tower undergoes a great repair during the reign of Sultan II. Mahmut (1808-1839). Maiden's Tower is mentioned in the various myths.

Anatolian Fortress

Ortaköy Mosque and Bosporus Bridge

Views from Dolmabahçe Palace

DOLMABAHCE PALACE

It is constructed between 1843-1856 during the reign of Sultan Abdülmecit. The architect of the Palace is Garabet Balyan. Palace, having an area with 110 000 square meters with its garden, is composed of three main buildings as Selamlık, Reception Hall and Harem. Unlike other sultan palaces, Selamlık and Harem of the palace are in the same building. The most important section of the palace is Reception (Ceremony) Hall. This hall is famous with the droplight in the weight of 4,5 tons. Dolmabahçe Palace is a version of baroque and rococo art nouveau, developing in Europe in 19th Century in terms of the ornamentation and decoration. Mustafa Kemal Atatürk starts alphabet revolution works in Republic period here. Turkish Language Councils are organized between 1927-1937 and II. Turkish History Congress is organized in 1937 here. Moreover, Ataturk died in this palace. Dolmabahçe Palace serves as a museum subject to Turkish Grand National Assembly National Palaces. Ihlamur Pavilion, located in Beşiktaş, is constructed by architect Nikogos Balyan by the order of sultan Abdülmecit between 1849 – 1855.

CIRAGAN PALACE

Sultan Abdulaziz gets the palace constructed between 1863-1866 . Plans and projects of the palace are prepared by Nikogos Balyan, construction of the palace is made by his sons Sarkis and Agop Balyan. Palace, witnessing the important historical events, is burned in 1910. Palace structure, which is not used for long period and remains empty, is turned into hotel by restoring in the recent times.

A View from Istanbul

YILDIZ PALACE

It is composed of structures group, located on the hillside between Beşiktaş and Ortaköy and constructed in the various times. Structures, which are built during the reign of Sultan Abdülaziz and II. Abdülhamit, are constructed in the different style because they are the works of different architects. Great Mabeyn, Small Mabeyn, Cit Pavilion, Yaveranlar office, Arsenal and Harem structures and theatre are some of these structures. There are a lot of kiosks in the garden of palace. The most important one is Şale kiosk, which is constructed by the order of II. Abdulhamit in honor of German Emperor in 1889.

Bosporus Bridge, which connects two continents to each other and is opened for transportation in 1973, and Fatih Sultan Mehmet Bridge, which is opened for transportation in 1988, are located on Istanbul Strait. Waterside residences, which are the most magnificent models of civil architecture works, are stood in line along the coast at two sides of the Bosporus.

BEYLERBEYI PALACE

Palace, which is located in Kuzguncuk, in Anatolian side, is constructed by the order of sultan Abdülaziz between 1862-1865. The architect of the palace is Serkis Balyan. Palace with three floors is composed of harem and selamlik sections. Küçüksu Pavilion, located in Göksu, is constructed in 1857. Its inner ornament and decoration belongs to French Sechan. The architect of the pavilion is Nikogos Balyan.

ANATOLIAN FORTRESS

Anatolian Fortress, which is also called Guzelcehisar or Akcahisar, is constructed by the order of Yıldırım Bayezit in 1393. Fortress is strengthened with some additional structures during the reign of Mehmed the Conqueror.

RUMELIAN FORTRESS

It is constructed by the order of Mehmed the Conqueror in 1452. It is said that plan of fortress belongs to the architect Musliheddin Ağa. Three big towers in the fortress are constructed by the order of Halil Pasha, Saruca Pasha and Zaganos Pasha and they are called with their names. Walls and small towers, connected these towers to each other, are constructed under the survey of Mehmed the Conqueror. After conquest of Istanbul, Saruca Pasha tower is turned into the state jailhouse. Fortress is abandoned because it losses its importance completely in 19th Century. It undergoes a great repair between 1953-1958 years. It is opened for public visits in 1958.

SAKIP SABANCI MUSEUM

Ottoman period calligraphy samples, decorative article, porcelain, furniture, picture, carpet and pictures of Turkish painters for Ottoman and Republic period and also, works of European painters, who live within boundaries of Ottoman boundaries are exhibited in the museum, located in Emirgan.

SADBERK HANIM MUSEUM

The most excellent works of Anatolian ethnography and archaeology are exhibited in the museum, located in Sarıyer and composed of two wooden waterside residences.

ADALAR (PRINCES' ISLANDS)

Adalar is the place where princes were exiled in Eastern Roman period and called Princes' Islands and known as Kınalıada, Burgazada, Heybeliada, Büyükada ve Sedef Island nowadays and there are some houses, kiosks and church structures, which are the most beautiful samples of civil architecture.

Burgaz Island

Views from Selimiye Mosque

Selimiye Mosque Inside and a View from Kırkpınar

EDIRNE

Edirne, which is a border city, is the gate of Turkey, which opens to Europe. Old name of Edirne, which is established by Roman emperor Hadrianus, is Hadrianopolis. Name of Edirne is derived from Hadrianopolis. First settlements in and around Edirne date back B.C. 4000 years. There is no important work, belonging to Roman and Byzantine periods, in the city. The city, which was conquered by Ottomans in 1363, becomes capital city until conquest of Istanbul. There are many works, belonging to Ottoman period, in the city. We can list them as follows. New Palace and Fatih Bridge in Sarayiçi location, where Kırkpınar oil-wrestling are organized traditionally every year, Rüstempaşa Hostel, which is constructed by Sinan the Architect in 1561 inside the city and Ali Pasha Grand Bazaar, built in 1569 and also Ahmet Pasha Hostel, Ottoman Bazaar, Tashan (Stone Khan), Yıldırım Bayezit Mosque (1397), Old Mosque (1414), Gazi Mihal Mosque and Bridge (1422); II. Bayezit Mosque and Hospital and School of Medicine (1488) within a social complex; Mosque with three minaret balconies, built during the reign of II. Murat (1421-1451) are some of the important works, located in the city. However, the most important work in Edirne is Selimiye Mosque, which is the symbol of the city and located in a social complex and built by famous architect, Sinan the Architect between 1569-1575 for the name of Sultan II. Selim and also is called "this is a work of my mastership period" by Sinan the Architect. Mosque has a wonderful appearance from afar with its dome in the diameter of 31,30 m and with its four minarets. İznik tiles of 16th Century decorate the niche and Sultan Mess of the mosque.

Great Mosque- Bursa

BURSA

City is established under the name of Prusa between B.C. 229-182 by Bithynia King I. Prusias and it is named as Bursa within elapsed time. City, which is captured by Romans in B.C. 74, is conquered by Ottomans in 1326 and becomes capital city in 1335. City, located in the foothill of Uludağ, is endowed with important architectural structures in the Ottoman period. There are many works, belonging to Ottoman period, in the city. A social complex, composed of mosque, madrasah, hamam and hospital, is constructed during the reign of Yildirim Bayezit in 1399 in the place, where is called "Yildirim Hill" nowadays; and also Ulu Mosque, which is the first and biggest mosque of Ottomans, is constructed in 1396-1400 years during the reign of Yildirim Bayezit. There are mosque and madrasah within the social complex, constructed by architect Hacı İvaz Pasha by the order of Celebi Mehmet in 1419 in Yesil location. Madrasah serves as Ethnography Museum nowadays. Yesil Tomb (1421), belonging

Great Mosque, Inside – Bursa

to Sultan Celebi Mehmet and constructed in 1421, is lo cated next to the mosque. There are mosque, madrasah, hamam, soup kitchen and tomb within the social complex, constructed by the order of Sultan II. Murat in Muradiye location. There are 12 tombs, in which dynasty members are buried, in the courtyard of the mosque. Tombs of Ottoman sultans Osman Bey (1299-1324) and Orhan Bey (1324-1362) are situated within the park in Tophane. I. Murat Hüdavendigar Mosque and Madrasah are located in Çekirge location, which is famous with the thermal springs. Furthermore, Tomb of Sultan I. Murat, who is martyred by a Serbian in the battle area in 1389, is also located here. Moreover, Ottoman House, Atatürk Kiosk, Archeological Museum and Uludağ, which is skiing center, are some of the visitation places in Bursa.

IZNIK / Niceae

Çakırca, Üyücek, Çicekli and Karadin tumuluses, located around Iznik, which is a county of Bursa, show that first settlements here, date back B.C. 2500 years. City is established under the name of Antigoneia in B.C. 316 by Antigonos, who is one of the commanders of Alexander the Great. Then, Lysimakhos names the city as Niceae due to the name of his wife. City enters under Roman rule in B.C. II. Century and first Consul meeting is organized here in 325 in the christianity period. Kutalmısoglu Suleyman captures the city in 1078 and it becomes the capital city. City passes under the control of Byzantines again in 1097 during I. Crusade. After Latins capture Istanbul during 4th Crusade in 1204, empire center of Byzantine is moved to Iznik and İznik becomes the capital city of Byzantine State until 1261. Iznik is captured during the reign of Sultan Orhan Bey in 1331 and includes into the boundaries of Ottoman Beylic. City is surrounded with walls, belonging to Roman and Byzantine periods, in the length of 4427m with 114 bastions and in th height of 10-13 m. It has four monumental ports, composed of Istanbul Gate, Lefke Gate, Yenisehir Gate ve Lake Gate. Theatre, constructed in the period of emperor Traianus (A.D. 98-117) and Hagia Sophia Church, constructed in IV. Century, are located within the city. Church is turned into the mosque in 1331 and it is opened for public visits as monumental museum in these days. Furthermore, the important structures are remains of Coimesis Church, constructed in 11th Century and Hagios Trifanos Church, constructed after 11th Century, Baptisterium of VI. Century and Senate Palace remains in the lake coast; Berberkaya Grave Monument and Aqueducts in the east of city; Beştaş Monument (Obelisk) around Elbeyli, Underground Grave Chamber (Hypoge) and Dört Tepeler Tumuluses. Some of other works, located in the county are 1333/34 dated Haci Ozbek Mosque, belonging to Ottoman period, 1378/91 dated Yesil Mosque, 1442/43 dated Mahmut Celebi Mosque, Nilufer Hatun Soup Kitchen, constructed in 1388 and serving as museum nowadays, 1332 dated Suleyman Pasa Madrasah, Yakup Celebi Small dervish lodge and Tomb, Big Hamam, belonging to period of I. Murat, Haci Hamza Hamam, belonging to period of II. Murat, Ismail Bey Hamam, belonging to 14th Century and also Sarı Saltuk Tomb, Kırgızlar Tomb, tombs of Çandarlı Hayrettin, Ibrahim and Halil Pashas, Huysuzlar Tomb, Ahiveyn Tomb, Alaattin-i Mısri and Davud-u Kayseri Tomb, Abdulvahap Sancaktari Tomb. Iznik is famous with its tiles. The oldest and most beautiful models at the construction tile-making domain of Ottoman ceramic art are produced in Iznik tile workshops. Tile art in Iznik peaks and it lives its prime period in 16th Century. Many tile workshops, established in Iznik nowadays, attempt to keep the tile art alive.

Green Mosque – İznik (Nicaea)

Troy-A View from the Historical City

ÇANAKKALE

Troy-A View from the Historical City

First settlement started by beginning from B.C. IV. Thousand, around Çanakkale Province, located in Anatolian side of the strait, which is called with its own name, and connecting Sea of Marmara and Aegean Sea to each other. The oldest settlement place is Troia. There are important ancient cities such as Assos, Alexandria Troas, Khrysa in the vicinity other than Troia. It witnesses great land and sea wars, which are made between Entente Powers, demanding to pass through Dardanelles Strait and Ottoman army under the commandership of Mustafa Kemal in 1915 during The First World War, and concluded with success of Ottoman army. Çimenlik, Kilitbahir, Bigalı and Nara, Çamburun and Karaburun, and Seddülbahir and Kumkale Castles are situated in two sides of the Strait, having an important position strategically. Canakkale Museum, in which archaeological and ethnographic works are exhibited, is one of the places, which are required to be visited. Gallipoli Peninsula, witnessing The First World War in 1915, has been declared as National Park in 1973. Canakkale Martyrs Monument is located in the southern end of Peninsula. Martyrs Monument Museum is situated under this monument. There are twelve martyrdoms in the peninsula. There are also monument and cemeteries of foreign soldiers.

TROIA

It is known as (W) Ilion-Wilus in Hittite language. It is an old historical city, comprising 9 layers in the height of 20 m. and located in Hisarlık district in 30 km southern west of Canakkale Province. It is demolished and established again for nine times in the history. First settlement here dates back B.C. 3000 years. Troia creats Bronze Age Civilization from B.C. 3000 to B.C. 1250, it lives Iron Age between B.C.1250 – B.C.1000 years. Troia is destroyed during campaign of Peoples of the Sea in B.C. 1200 and its period, passing until B.C. 700, is dark. This period is not known. At the end of this period, Troia is constructed onto old Troia by the residents of Asia Minor again. VI. Floor of Troia is mentioned in Iliad Epopee of Homer and witnesses the wars about B.C. 1240. Roman period starts in Troia in B.C. 85. Roman emperors accept that their origins are based on Trojans and pay special attention and give special importance to Troia. They are interested closely in the city and equip it with the architectural structures. Even Constantine the Great intends to move capital city Roma to Troia in (306-337) A.D. 4th Century. Life quality in Troia starts to fall back by beginning from 6th Century. Life finishes in the city in the 1st thousand year and it starts to play the role of the site. Remains of VI. Troia Walls (B.C. 1800-1275), Megaron houses, and also, Temple of Athena, used between B.C. 350-A.D.400 years, Great Theatre, sanctuary, Monumental Fountain (nymphaeum), small theatre and assembly building (bouleterion) can be seen in Troia site. First excavation in Troia is started by Henrich Schliemann in 1870. He assumes that valuable works, which he finds during the excavation, are the treasures, belonging to Troia king Priamos and he takes them and escapes there. While these works are exhibited in Berlin Museum, Russians occupy Berlin during The Second World War and they collect these works and they take them away to Moscow. These works are still located in Pushkin Museum in Moscow. Mount Ida (Kaz Mountain), located within boundaries of Canakkale Province, is the place, where the first beauty contest is organized in the world history. This beauty contest causes the occurrence of Trojan War due to its results. According to the myth, goddess of vengeance Eris is not invited by gods, to the wedding of Peleus and Thetis, which is organized in Mount Olympus, in order not to stir up trouble. Goddess Eris, who is angry with this, throws a golden apple, on which it is written as "to three beautifuls", in front of head god Zeus. Zeus can not

Troy-A View from the Historical City

Assos

decide to which goddess he shall give such apple. Therefore, he appoints Paris, who is the son of Troia king Priamos, living in Mount Ida, as arbitrator. Hera, Athena and Aphrodite, who are the goddesses, claiming to be beautiful, participate into the contest. All goddesses promise to make great donations to Paris in order to ensure him to give golden apple to them. However, Paris gives the golden apple to Aphrodite, promising the most beautiful woman of the worldwide to him. Then Paris sees the beautiful Helena during his voyage to Isparta and falls in love with him. Aphrodite fills heart of Helena with love flame for Paris in accordance with her promise to Paris. Thereupon, Paris takes Helena, who is the beautiful wife of Menelaos, one of Akhaioi brave men and escapes with her to Troia. Thereupon, Akhaioi start Trojan War.

ASSOS / Behramkale

Assos ancient city is located on a hill, between Tuzla Stream (Satnioeis) and sea, near Ayvacik county, Behramkale village. City enters under the rule of Lydians by beginning from B.C. 560, Persians in B.C. 546, Macedonian Empire in B.C. 334, Kingdom of Pergamon in B.C. 241, Roman Empire in B.C. 133, Eastern Roman Empire in 395 respectively. Assos (Behramkale) includes into Ottoman territories during the reign of I. Murat (1362-1389). Famous philosopher Aristoteles provides philosophy courses in Assos for three years periods between B.C. 348-345 years. City is established on a hill, dominating the sea and land, and walls and gates, belonging to B.C. 4th Century and surrounding the city, have an authentic architecture workmanship. Main entrance gate of the city is in the west. Furthermore, there are also secondary gates. Temple of Athena (B.C. 530), located in Acropolis, is in the dor order and with 6 x 13 columns and is the temple, which is built with the oldest dor order in Western Anatolia. There is also Murat Hüdavendigar Mosque, constructed during the reign of Ottoman sultan I. Murat, in Acropolis. North stoa of Agora, constructed probably in B.C. 3rd Century and located in the south of Acropolis, has two floors and is constructed in the dor order. Covered bazaar and stoa of Agora with three floors are located in the south. Moreover, there is a small temple in Agora. Bouleuterion structure is situated in the east of Agora. There is a gymnasion structure, belonging to B.C. 2nd Century, in the northern west of Agora. Theatre building, constructed in B.C. 3rd Century and modified in Roman Age, is located in

Views from Pergamon

Pergamon

the south of Agora. Necropolis area is located outside city walls and in teh west of Acropolis. Also, remains of wave breaker can be seen in Assos port. There is a bridge, belonging to Ottoman period and constructed in 14th Century, on Tuzla Stream (Satnioeis) in the North of ancient city.

BERGAMA/Pergamon

City, which is called Pergamon in antique age, was a small settlement place in early times. When Lysimakhos, dominating Anatolian part from divided empire lands by beginning from B.C. 301 after the death of Alexander the Great in B.C. 323, is dead in B.C. 284, one of his commanders, Philetairos establishes Kingdom of Pergamon (B.C. 283-133) in B.C. 283. Philetairos (B.C. 283-263) extends territories of the kingdom until Sea of Marmara. One of his sequent kings, I. Eumenes (B.C. 263-241) wages war with Galatians, Bergama is furnished with the most magnificent structures in the period of I. Attalos (241-197), II. Eumenes (197-159) turns the kingdom into a powerful state, and he broadens his lands to Taurus Mountains. He transforms the city to the culture and art center, and he establishes a rich library and furnishes the city with the most magnificent structures. Bergama becomes the model city of that period in terms of architecture and sculpture. Later on, II. Attalos (159-138) and then III. Attalos (138-133) takes the head. After III. Attalos donates the kingdom to Roman Empire in B.C. 133, Kingdom of Pergamon expires. Bergama survives as an important center in Roman Age. It becomes episcopalism center in the Christianty period; city is surrounded with walls in Byzantine period again. City, occupied by Arabians in 8th Century, is captured by Ottomans in 1330. We can review Pergamon ruins in three sections as Acropolis, Roman city at the lowland and Sanctuary of Asclepius. Heroon, which is constructed as area of worshipping to Pergamon kings, is located in the left before arriving to great castle gate, outside the original castle in Acropolis. Only foundations of Temple of Athena in Sanctuary of Athena within the castle, reach today. Temple is constructed in the dor order at the beginning of B.C. 3rd Century and has 6 x 10 columns.

Pergamon

There were stoas with two floors in the northern and eastern direction of Sanctuary of Athena and there was Propylon structure, which was an entrance structure in the east. The greatest library of ancient age, containing 200.000 volumes of books, was located in the east of northern stoa. There were palaces of Pergamon kings in the eastern of the library. There were arsenals, which are military material depot, in the northern end of the Acropolis. There was a Temple of Traian, constructed on a terrace in Roman Age, in Acropolis. Temple is constructed on the corinthian order and it is a structure with 6 x 9 columns. Emperor Hadrianus (118-137) gets the temple constructed for emperor Traianus (98-117), who Emperor Hadrianus becomes emperor instead. Pergamon Theatre, constructed on a steep slope in B.C. 3rd Century, is modified in Roman Age. Theatre, having 10.000 audience capacity, is the steepest theatre of the world. Temple of Dionysos, located at northern end of the theatre's terrace, is constructed in B.C. 2nd Century but it is renewed during the period of emperor Caracalla (211-217) in Roman Age. Zeus Altar is situated at the south of Athena's terrace. Altar is constructed in B.C. 190 in memory of the war, which is won against Galatians during the period of II. Eumenes. The war between gods and giants is depicted in the frieze, decorated with high reliefs, in the length of 120 meters. Zeus Altar, brought into the open during the excavations in 1878, is moved to Berlin with the consent of Sultan Abdülhamit (1876-1909) and exhibited in Pergamon Museum there by erecting it. Upper Agora is located immediately under Zeus Altar. There is a small temple, belonging to Hermes, who is god of commerce in Agora. Temple of Demeter, Temple of Hera, Temple of Asclepeion, Gymnasium, are located in middle city; Council Attalos House, lower agora and Eumenes II Gate are located in lower city. The biggest and the oldest structure in Bergama is Temple of Serapis, which is constructed during the period of emperor Hadrianus (117-138) and consecrated to gods of Egypt, and called Red Basilica in these days. Temple is turned into the church in the Christianity period. Theatre, stadium and amphitheatre in lower city are constructed in Roman period. Maltepe and Yığmatepe tumulus are located in the lowland. Health Hostel of Asclepius, which is called Sanctuary of Asclepius, is established in B.C. 4th Century and it becomes one of the most famous health center of that period in A.D. 2nd Century in Roman age. Patients are used to be treated with inculcation, clearance, drinking cure, mud, water and sun baths, theatre plays, concert, drugs made of healing herbs here. It is used to be arrived to Asclepius from the city in Roman age by passing through 1 km colonnaded street, called Via Tecta. Health Hostel of Asclepius is an open area, with three parts, surrounded with galleries. There are propylon courtyard and propylon building, area, where religious ceremonies are organized, structures such as Temple of Asclepius, libraries, stoas, chamber of sleep, fountains, pools, a tunnel opening to treatment structures, women and men toilets, meeting and conference hall within this area and; there is a theatre building for 3500 people, placed on a hillside at its northern west corner. Famous physician Galenos, living in Roman Age, is from Bergama.Archeological excavations in Bergama are started by German engineer Karl Humann in 1878. After the first excavations, made in Acropolis, excavations are ceased during the First and Second World Wars. Archeological excavations in Bergama are carried out by German scientists in these days. Works, unearthed from excavations, are exhibited in Bergama Museum. A second Health Hostel (Asclepius), belonging to god of healing in Anatolia, is unearthed as a result of excavations, made on Allianoi ancient city, located in Pasa Ilıcası district in the vicinity of Bergama recently. However, Allianoi ancient city faces with danger of submerging into Yortanlı Dam under construction unfortunately.

SARDES

Antique Sardes site, which is the capital city of Lydia Kingdom, is located in the vicinity of Salihli county, in Manisa Province. Coin is minted in this city by Lydians in B.C. 7th Century for the first time in the history. "Royal Road", starting from Susa, which is a city of Persian Empire in Iran, finished in Sardes. This road is in the length of 2575 km. City lives its most prime period in B.C. 7th and 6th Century. Great public works are made in the city in Hellenistic and Roman ages. The first archeological excavations in Sardes are made by USA scientists between 1910-1914 years and unearthed works are moved to America and exhibited

Sard (Sardes)

Sard (Sardes)

in Metropolitan Museum in New York. Excavations here are ceased for long period and excavations are started again by USA scientists in 1958. Today, works unearthed from Sardes excavations, are exhibited in Manisa Museum. Temple of Artemis in Sardes ancient city are constructed in three stages. Its first stage coincides to B.C. 300, second stage coincides to B.C. 175-150 and three stage, coincides to A.D. 150. Cella of the temple is divided into two parts with a wall in such final stage, while this section is consecrated to goddess Artemis, other section is presented to Faustina, who is wife of Roman Emperor Antoninus Pius (138-161) and divinized after her death and it is turned into a worshipping area. Architectural remains in the vicinity of the southeastern corner of the temple belong to a church, constructed in A.D. 4th Century. The other important structures in Sardes ancient city are Synagogue and Gymnasium, restored and constructed in A.D. III. Century; Theatre and Stadium, constructed in B.C. 300 and modified in Roman Age, and also Byzantine Church, House with Bronze are some of the other architectural remains in the ancient city. There are hundreds of tumulus belonging to Lydian period at the lowland between Sardes and Lake of Marmara. Lydia Kingdom comes into existence with king Giges (B.C. 680-652) in B.C. 680. Lydians enter under Persian rule after Kroisos (B.C.575-546) is beaten by Persian King II. Kyrus (B.C. 559-529) in 546. They live under Persian rule within the period, passing until B.C. 333 when Alexander the Great beats Persian King III. Dareius (B.C. 336-330). Lydian Civilization survives until B.C. 300.

Izmir, which is a port city along Aegean Sea, is the biggest city of Aegean Region and it is the third biggest city of Turkey and also it is the trade, art and culture center of the region. City, which is called Smyrna in Ancient age, is the birth place of Homer, who is author of Epopee of Iliad and Odyssey, at the same time. Smyrna is known as Tismurna – Smurna in Hittite language. Excavations, made on Bayraklı tumulus, show that first settlement here dates back B.C. 3000 years. Smyrna city enters under the rules of respectively Lydians in B.C. 600, Persians in B.C. 546, Alexander the Great in B.C. 334. New city is established in Kadifekale piedmonts during the reign of Alexander the Great. Peoples of old city are moved to here. City is spread into a large area from Kadifekale to the port in B.C. I. Century and is furnished with various architectural structures such as temple, theatre, stadium, gymnasium, agora. Strabon says that Smyrna is the most beautiful city of Ionia region in this century. Only remains of State agora and antique aqueducts reach today among these structures. High embossed depictures of Poseidon and Demeter, which are located in the middle of Agora and made of marble, are moved into the museum. There are Archaeology Museum, Agora Open Air Museum, Atatürk Museum, Ethnography Museum, Picture and Sculpture Museum in Izmir.

Watch Tower-İzmir (Smyrna)

EFES / EPHESUS

City of Ephesus is a port city, established along Aegean Sea, where Küçük Menderes river flows into the sea in B.C. 10th century. Ephesus is known as Apasas in Hittite language. Ephesus is ruled respectively by Cimmerians in B.C. 7th Century and Lydians in the middle of B.C. 6th Century. Ephesus, captured by Persians in B.C. 546, enters under the rules of respectively Macedonian Empire in B.C. 334, Seleucians in B.C. 323, Kingdom of Pergamon in B.C. 190, Roman Empire in B.C. 133. City lives its most prime period in Roman Age and its population exceeds 200.000. City witnesses important events in the Christianity period. City is moved to Ayasoluk Hill, where Selçuk county, is located, due to filling the port with alluvial soils, brought by Küçük Menderes river in A.D. 6th Century and Arabian invasions in 7th Century. Ephesus lives its last period in Anatolian Seljuk Empire period and it losses its importance in the Ottoman period. City remains about 7 km far from the sea today due to filling the port with alluvial soils, brought by Küçük Menderes river. First excavation works in Ephesus are started by English archaeologist J. T. Wood in 1869 and he brings into open remains of Temple of Artemis in Ephesus, which is one of Seven Wonders of the Ancient Age. Temple, constructed in B.C. 6th Century, is burned in B.C. 356. Temple is reconstructed in the same place again in B.C. 4th Century. Temple is destroyed substantially in A.D. 5th Century. Foundation stones and pulleys of a column reach today from this temple. Austria scientists start Ephesus site excavations in 1895. Excavations are ceased due to the First (1914-1918) and Second (1939-1945) World Wars. Excavations are still carried out by Austrian scientists in these days. Works, unearthed from the excavations, are exhibited in Ephesus Museum in Selçuk County. There is a castle, constructed in the Christianity period in Ayasuluk Hill in Selçuk and fortified substantially in Seljuk period. There is also St. Jean Church of great Christian saint and the Bible author, which is constructed by the order of Emperor I. Iustinianos (A.D. 527-565) on this hill. Grave of St. Jean is also located under this church. The important structure, whose construction is completed in 1375, is Isa Bey Mosque, which is located on this hill and the structure of Aydınoğlu Beylic period.

Hadrianus – Ephesus (Back Page)

Selam sana
Allah'ın en sevgili kulu Meryem
Rab seninledir
Kadınların en mübareği sensin
ve mübarektir senin evladın
İsa
Aziz Meryem, Mesih'in annesi,
biz günahkârlar için,
şimdi ve ölüm
dua eyle

Virgin Mary

A View from Historical City of Ephesus

When it is turned from Selçuk – Kuşadası turnout, and entered into Ephesus ancient city, there are Vedius Gymnasium, made by a rich man from Ephesus in A.D. 150 and stadium, constructed during the period of Emperor Nero, in the left; and Byzantine Baths, constructed in A.D. 6th Century, The Virgin Mary Church, belonging to A.D. 4th Century, and then Port Gymnasium and Baths, whose construction is started by emperor Domitian and completed in the period of emperor Hadrian, in the right. Structure of Theatre Gymnasium, constructed in A.D. 2nd Century, is located in the east of Port Gymnasium. Colonnaded street, opened into the port, is Arcadian Avenue, constructed in Hellenistic period. This avenue is called with this name because it is reconstructed during the period of emperor Arcadias (395-408). A fountain, belonging to Hellenistic period, is located in the eastern end of this avenue. Theatre building, constructed in Hellenistic period and with 24.000-people capacity, is modified and enlarged with some outbuildings during the period of emperor Claudius (41-54), Nero (54-68) and Trajan (98-117) in Roman Age. Marble road passes at the direction of north-south from the front of theatre. Commercial Agora, which is constructed in Hellenistic period and enlarged with outbuildings during the period of emperor Augustus and Nero in Roman Age and restored during the period of emperor Caracalla, is located in the west of marble road. Agora's southern-east gate with three passages is opened into the square, where Library of Celsus is situated. Library of Celsus, erected by restoring its front in 1978, is constructed between A.D. 110-135 years. Front of library, constructed with two floors, was containing rich architectural decorations. Temple of Serapis, belonging to an Egyptian god and located at the direction of west gate of Commercial Agora, must have been constructed in Antonians Period (138-192) probably. Kuretler Avenue is the avenue, starting in front of Library of Celsus and extending to State Agora. Baths, located in the left of this avenue and constructed in A.D. 100 years, is restored by a Christian woman, named as Scholastic in 4th century and called after this name.

Here is also known as Love Home at the same time. Temple of Hadrian, constructed in the Corinthian order for the name of emperor Hadrian (117-138), is located in the left along the avenue after these baths and Hillside Houses, constructed in A.D. 1st Century and, used during centuries and belonging to rich men from Ephesus, are located in the right of the avenue. Fountain of Trajan, constructed during the period of emperor Trajan (98-117) and then remains of entrance gate, embossed with Heracles, and monument, erected for the name of Memmius, grandson of Dictator Sulla, are located in the left of avenue. Temple of Domitian, constructed between 81-96, on a terrace, is located in the right side. State Agora is located at the end of Kuretler Avenue. There are Prytaneion, Odeon and special baths in the north of State Agora; and a monumental fountain, constructed in A.D. 2nd Century, in the south. Eastern Gymnasium and remains of Magnesia Gate, which is entrance gate of the city in this direction and constructed during the period of emperor Vespasian (69-79), are located in more eastern side. It is said that The Virgin Mary spends her last days in Bulbul Mount in Ephesus region and dies here. "House of The Virgin Mary" in this mount becomes place of pilgrimage for Christians after visitation of Pope Paul VI in 1967. Main goddess of Ephesus is Artemis. When St. Paul comes to Ephesus in A.D. I. Century and carries out missionary activities, he gets great reaction of domestic peoples and he is obliged to escape from the city as a result of occurred riot. However, belief in Jesus and The Virgin Mary takes the place of belief in Artemis, in the course of time in Ephesus. Cave of Seven Sleepers, which is the important place in the Christianity belief, is located in the side of Panayir Mount, facing to the lowland at the direction of northern-east of Ephesus. Furthermore, Şirince, which is an old Greek village and located in 7 km far from Selçuk county, shows important developments in terms of tourism in the recent years.

Artemis Statue-Ephesus

A View from Historical City of Ephesus

The House of Virgin Mary

Traian Fountain

Celsius Library

Seljuk Castle

Kuşadası (Bird Island)

KUŞADASI

Kuşadası, which is coastal county subject to Aydın province, is one of the most important tourism centers in Aegean Region. Kuşadası port is the haunt of great ships of international touristic travel agencies due to Ephesus, Priene, Miletus, Didima around it and even historical places such as Pamukkale and Aphrodisias, located far from it, and also House of Virgin Mary. Marina, constructed in the recent years and great touristic facilities, constructed around it, increase the importance of Kuşadası much more and become the county and its surrounding as a great tourism center. First settlements in Kuşadası date back B.C. 3rd Century. Neapolis, which is located in the south of county and a summer resort of Ephesus in Roman Age, is the first settlement place. City, which is ruled by Venice and Genoeses in Middle Age, is moved into its current place and called Scala Nova (New Port). Kuşadası is participated into Ottoman lands during the period of Çelebi Mehmet and its name is originated from Güvercinada next to it. Güvercinada is surrounded with walls as it is used as the military base in Byzantine period. Works before Ottoman period are not seen in Kuşadası. Grand Vizier Öküz Mehmet Pasha gets a hostel and a mosque constructed in Kuşadası in 1618. Furthermore, he gets Kuşadası surrounded with walls having three gates in order to protect from pirates. Öküz Mehmet Pasha Hostel, serving as motel after restoration, and Kaleiçi Mosque and a tower, belonging to old walls, used as military guard post, reach today. No remains of walls reach today. Old Kuşadası Houses are located within the castle. Castle in Güvercinada undergoes repair in 1834 in order to be used as outpost by Ottomans.

PRIENE

Priene ancient city is located in Güllübahçe village, subject to Söke county. Priene, which is a port city in the seaside in advance, is moved into current place because of filling the sea with soils, brought by Big Menderes. This city is establishes in B.C. 350 years. Firstly, city enters under Kingdom of Pergamon rule and then it is ruled by Roman Empire in B.C. 133. City starts to loss its importance by beginning from A.D. 3rd Century and becomes bishopric center in the Christianity period. City is constructed by dividing avenues which

Theater Priene

pass each other vertically, into constituted squares according to plan of famous architect Hippodamus. City was surrounded with walls. City had the most beautiful architectural structures of Hellenistic Period. The first archeological excavations in Priene are started by Carl Humann in 1895 and continue until 1898. Temple of Athena is the most important architectural structure of the city and it is constructed between B.C. 350-325 years. It is the work of famous architect Pytheos. Temple, constructed in Ion order, has 6 x 11 columns. Construction of temple is contributed by Alexander the Great. Some columns of the temple are erected. Agora, surrounded with stoas from three sides, is located in the city center and constructed in B.C. 3rd Century. Temple of Zeus, located in the east of Agora, is a structure, built in Ion order in B.C. 3rd Century. Bouleuterion, which is one of the best protected structures of Priene, has a capacity of 640 people and is constructed in B.C. 150. Structure of Prytaneion is located adjacent to this structure. Theatre building is one of the best protected structures and is constructed in the second half of B.C. 4th Century and undergoes repair in Roman Period. City has two great gymnasiums, of which one is in the north and the other is in the south. Temple in Sanctuary of Demeter in the north of city, is the oldest temple of Priene and it is presented to goddess Demeter and Kore. Temple of Kybele and House of Alexander are located in a place in the vicinity of Western Gate of City and a Byzantine basilica structure is located in the south of theatre.

MILET / MILETUS

Miletus, which is a port city in the place where Büyük Menderes river flows into Aegean Sea in Archaic Age, remains very far from the sea at the present because of filling the sea with alluvial soils, brought by the river. First

Theater -Milet

settlements here date back B.C. 2000 years. City gets rich very much due to colonies, established in Mediterranean Sea and Black Sea. Miletus is known as Milavanda in Hittite language. It lives its most prime period in B.C. 7th and 6th Century. Foundations of positive sciences are laid in Miletus. All of philosophers of nature such as Thales, Anaximenes, Anaximander, historian and geographer Hecate, city planner architect Hippodamus, architect of Hagia Sophia Isidore are from Miletus. Thales calculates solar eclipse in B.C. 585 in advance and informs it to the people. Miletus city rebels against Persian Empire and burns the freedom torch in the Western Anatolia. However, it could not be successful. After Persians, occupying the city in B.C. 494, rob all treasuries both in Miletus and also in Didima, they set city of Miletus, the leader of riot, up on fire and destroy it. After Persians demolish city of Miletus completely, Hippodamos prepares a proper plan for city of Miletus. City is occupied by Alexander the Great in B.C. 334. City witnesses the public works in Hellenistic and Roman ages. City losses its importance in Byzantine period because of filling the sea with alluvial soils, brought by Büyük Menderes river. The first archeological excavations in Miletus are started by German Th. Wiegand in 1899. Excavations are ceased during the First and Second World Wars. Excavations are carried out again by German scientists in these days. Works, unearthed from excavations, are exhibited in Milet Museum. The most magnificent structure of the city is the theatre. Theatre, constructed in B.C. 4th Century, is enlarged in Hellenistic period and while it has a capacity with 3500 people, its capacity is increased to 15.000 people in Roman age. Hill, on which theatre is located, is surrounded with walls and turned into a castle in Byzantine period. There is a hostelry, belonging to 15th Century, in the plain place in front of theatre. Bouleuterion building, constructed between B.C. 175-164, had a capacity with 1500 people. South Agora is constructed in A.D. 2nd Century and its North Gate, which is unearthed during the excavations, is moved to Berlin and it is erected again and exhibited in Pergamon Museum there. Baths, which are constructed by the order of II. Faustina, who is wife of Emperor Marcus Aurelius, and called with her own name, are in the best protected position. North Agora structure, constructed in the classical period, is enlarged in Hellenistic and Roman periods. Delphinion structure, which is constructed in Hellen

Apollo Temple-Didim

istic period and modified in Roman age, is consecrated to Delphinion (dolphin), which is sacred animal of god Apollo. Gymnasium, constructed in A.D. 2nd Century, is composed of propylon and five reading chambers and one palestra. Great Port Monument, constructed in B.C. 31, is erect in the memory of emperor Augustus, winning Action war. Stadium, constructed in B.C. 150, is enlarged in Roman age and its capacity is increased to 15.000 people. Temple of Serapis, belonging to A.D. III. Century, West Agora belonging to Hellenistic period, Roman Baths, belonging to A.D. I. century, Bishop Church belonging to A.D. 5th Century, Nymphaion, constructed in A.D. 2nd Century, Capito Baths, constructed in Emperor Claudius (41-54) period, Temple of Athena, belonging to B.C. 5th Century, Temple of Asclepius and Synagogue are some of the other important structures in the city. Isa Bey Mosque, constructed in 1404, is one of the most beautiful models of marble workmanship in Miletus site, which is called Balat in Seljuks period. Mosque, located within the social complex, composed of madrasah, soup kitchen and graveyard, is constructed by the order of Ottoman commander Ilyas Bey.

DIDIMA

Didima is located within boundaries of Eskihisar village, subject to Söke. Apollo temples, constructed in Didima in B.C. 8th and 7th century, were small and modest structures. Temple of Apollo becomes a great temple just in B.C. 6th century. Temple, constructed for the name of God Apollo, is the greatest prophecy center in Western Anatolia. The first great temple, constructed in Ion order between B.C. 560-550, was a dipteral structure in the sizes of 38,39 x 85,15m. There was an altar in the front section of temple. The new temple, constructed in B.C. 300, is third great temple, located in Aegean world, coming after Temple of Artemis in Ephesus and Temple of Hera in Samos. Architects of temple are Paionios from Ephesus and Daphnis from Miletus. Temple is in the size of 51,13 x 109,34m. Although it is greater than the old temple, the same plan is applied. There are total 120 columns, of which 108 double columns surround the temple and 12 columns located in the pronaos. Height of columns was about 19,70 m. Temple was located on a base with seven steps. Gryphon frieze in Aditon and cella walls and other god busts, head pieces, ornamented with bull and gryphon heads, friezes with decorated Medusa heads belong to the same period. Medusa reliefs, constituting

frieze on the outer column line of the temple, belong to A.D. II. Century. Stadium structure, in which religious ceremonies and sacred races are organized, are located in 15 m south of the temple. Temple is abandoned in the Christianity period. Church and some houses are constructed into the temple; Byzantines make barracks and military garrison. Temple, having many fires, is destroyed completely during the earthquake, occurred in 15th Century. A village is constituted around the temple by benefiting from remains of temple in 19th Century.

MILAS

Milas, which is known as "Milasa" in Archaic Age, is an important religious center as well as it becomes capital city of Caria region at the same time. The sightseeing works in the city are remains of extant Temple of Zeus from archaic age, in Hisarbaşı district of Milas, traces of Baltalı Gate and city walls and Gümüşkesen Memorial Tomb. Lion sculpture on Gumuskesen Memorial Tomb is disassembled from its place by English archaeologist Newton and moved into British Museum in the middle of 19th Century. Architectural structures such as Hacı İlyas Bey Mosque (1330), belonging to Menteseoğulları period, Ulucami, Belen Mosque, converted from church to mosque, and Firuzbey Mosque, belonging to Ottoman period (at the end of 14th Century), Ağa Mosque (1737) and Çöllü Hostelry, Yanık Hostelry, Sünnetçi Hostelry, Caput Hostelry reach today. Peçin Castle, constructed in 14th Century by Menteseoğulları, is located in 5 km south of Milas. There are historical buildings such as Yelli Mosque, Ahmet Gazi Medresesi (1375) and Kizil Hostelry within this castle.

BODRUM / HALICARNASSUS

It is the most important tourism centers of Turkey. It is the starting place of famous "Blue Cruises", aiming to see unique natural beauties and historical richness, containing southern-west coasts of Aegean Region, lacy and wavy bays, coves and waterside thickets. Marina, constructed in the recent years and Milas-Bodrum Airport increase the importance of Bodrum in terms of tourism much more. Name of Bodrum is originated from word of St. Petrus. Bodrum is the changing version of word of St. Petrus in the course of time. Name of the city is Halicarnassus in Archaic Age. Famous his-

Bodrum

torian Herodot is from Halicarnassus. Mausoleum of Mausolus, which is constructed in the first age and one of seven wonders of the world, is located here. Relief and architectural pieces of this monument are used in the construction of St. Petrus Castle (Bodrum Castle), constructed in 1402 by Knights of Rhodes. Bodrum Castle undergoes a great repair in the Republic period and serves as Bodrum Underwater Archaeology Museum in these days. Works, unearthed from underwater excavations, are exhibited in this museum. Mausoleum of Mausolus: Mausoleum of Mausolus, which is one of seven architectural wonders of the ancient age, is constructed by the order of his wife Artemisia, for Mausolus in B.C. 350. Mausoleum is the opus of famous architect Pytheos. Mausoleum is located on the pyramid roof with 24 stairs, raising on 36 columns line, located on a high base and a cart with four horses having sculptures of Mausolus and Artemisia inside. Reliefs, decorating Mausoleum, are made by Scopas, Leochares, Bryaxis and Timotheos, who are famous sculptors of that period. English ambassador Lord Stratford has marble reliefs of monument, used in the construction of Bodrum Castle, disassembled from their places with the consent of Ottoman sultan, Sultan Abdülmecit (1839-1861) and carried to London in 1846; architectural pieces and sculptures and reliefs, which are unearthed as a result of excavations, made on the mausoleum by Newton in 1857, are carried to London by English people again with the consent of Sultan Abdülmecit and exhibited in worldwide famous British Museum. A theatre structure of Roman period is located along the main road, passing from top section of Bodrum county. Antique theatre undergoes repair substantially.Bodrum Castle (St. Petrus Castle): After Bodrum is captured by Knights of Rhodes in 1402,a castle is constructed on a rocky area in the form of peninsula, located between two ports, by Knights of Rhodes between 1415-1503 by the order of Pope dated 1409. Castle, having a square plan, is in the sizes of 180 m X 185 m. The highest tower of the castle is French Tower. Other towers are Italian Tower, German Tower, Serpent Tower and English Tower. Sections of castle, remaining out of eastern wall, are supported with the double main wall. After seven gate is passed, it is arrived to the citadel. There are emblems, containing cross, dragon and lion figures on the gates. Architectural pieces, sculptures and reliefs of Mausoleum of Mausolus, which is one of seven architectural wonders of the ancient age, are used in the construction of the castle. Castle is conquered by Ottomans in 1522 and used as jailhouse at the end of 19th Century.

Bodrum

Works, located in the collections of Bodrum Underwater Archaeology Museum, are exhibited in the locations, named as Turkish hamam, Amphora exhibition, Eastern Roman Ship, Glass Hall, Glass Shipwreck, Coin and Jewelry Hall, Carios Princess Hall, English Tower, Torture And Massacre Chambers an German Tower. Furthermore, many works are exhibited in the other outdoor locations of the castle.

MARMARİS

Marmaris, located in the seaside and around a bay and among greeneries, is a piece from paradise. It is in the position of an important tourism center in the last years. Its marina provides an important contribution to the city in terms of sea tourism. Physkos ancient city, located in front of the hill along western side of the city, is the oldest settlement place of the city. We can list old works, located in the city, as follows. Marmaris Castle, constructed in 11th century, undergoes repair during the reign of Kanuni Sultan Süleyman in 1557 and then ruined castle is repaired in the recent period and serves as Marmaris Museum in these days. Taşhan (Stone Hostelry), constructed again during the reign of Kanuni Sultan Süleyman and hostel, constructed in 1545, mosque, built by Ibrahim Aga in 1789, Değirmen Stream Bridge are the other important historical structures in the city. Many of old works in Marmaris are constructed by the order of Kanuni Sultan Süleyman, launching an expedition to Rhodes Island in 1522. There are numberless islands, caves, coves and sites, containing beauties for sightseeing around Marmaris. Some of them are Sedir Island, Hisarönü, English Port, Karacasöğüt, Alkaya Cave, Asarcıktepe.

DATÇA - CNIDUS

Datça, located in the peninsula situated between Gökova Bay and Hisarönü Bay and called with its own name, starts to be an attraction center in terms of tourism in the recent years. There is no considerable old structure in the county. The most important ancient city in Datça peninsula is Cnidus, which is a famous city of ancient age, and located in the western end of peninsula. Cnidus, constructed according to Hippodamus city plan and established on the terraces, had two ports, of which one is military. City, which a commercial center, plays an important role in the ancient world by beginning from B.C. 6th century. Cnidus is the city of goddess of beauty Aphrodite. Aphrodite sculpture, made by famous sculptor Praxiteles, who we know from copies of Roman Period, was situated in Temple of Aphrodite, located in Cnidus. Mathematician-astronomer Eudoxos, living in B.C. 400, is from Cnidus. Again, Sostratos, who is the architect of Lighthouse of Alexandria, which is one of seven wonders of the world, is from Cnidus. First excavation in Cnidus is made by C.T. Newton in 1857 and famous "Sitting Demeter Sculpture" is carried into British Museum in London with works, found in the excavation. Prof. Dr. I. C. Love from USA, makes excavations between 1967-1977 years and Prof. Dr. Ramazan Özgan carries out the excavation works since 1988. Walls surrounding the city date back B.C. 4th Century. Theatre of the city for 4500 people, Odeon and stoa, construction in dor order, belong to Hellenistic period. Temple of Dionysus dates back period of Roman emperor Hadrian and is constructed in the Corinthian order. Temple of Apollo Carneios, belonging to B.C. 2nd Century, Temple of Aphrodite, bouleuterion, which is the structure of Roman Age, upper theatre, modified in Roman period, basilica, Temple of Muses are some of the other ancient structures, located in the city.

Marmaris

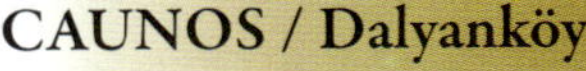

CAUNOS / Dalyanköy

Caunos ancient city, located within boundaries of Köyceğiz county and in the opposite shore of Dalyan Strait, is established by Caunos, one of twin children of Miletus according to the myth. Canuos, which is port city in Ancient Age, remains very far from the shore because of filling the port with alluvial soils, brought by Dalyan Stream. Rock tombs in the entrance of city are the attractive works for the visitors. On the other hand, walls in the length of 3 km surrounding the city; stoa, agora, Roman baths, palestra, Demeter terrace and temple, belonging to Hellenistic period; temple of Roman age, constructed in the Corinthian order, Vespasian fountain, theatre, constructed in Hellenistic Period but modified in Roman period, water tank, Aphrodite Eupolia Temple, Temple of Terrace, constructed in dor order, Temple and Sanctuary of Apollo, Heroon, Byzantine age church, are some of the other structure remains, located in the ancient city. City, having a considerably common settlement in Ancient, Classical, Hellenistic, Roman and Byzantine periods, is abandoned in A.D. century. Even though Upper

Datça-Knidos

Rock Tombs-Dalyan

Acropolis is fortified and used some time in the Middle Age, this settlement does not take long period. Dalyan Stream, arising from Köyceğiz Lake, meanders to the sea. As coast line is the spawning area of sea turtles, called Caretta Caretta, it is under protection.

GÖCEK

Göcek, which is the single settlement area located in the northern end of Gulf of Fethiye, is a sweet town, containing natural beauties. It has a much more important position in terms of tourism with its marina, constructed in the recent years. Göcek is third degree natural site area and located within a specially protected environment area. Göcek Island, Yilanli Island, Zeytinli Island, Tersane Island, Domuz Island and Akbük, Boynuz Waterside Thicket, beautiful coves such as Bedri Rahmi Cove, Sıralıbük, Sarsala Cove, Manastır Cove, Göbün Cove, located within the bay, are the unique places, required to be visited.

FETHİYE

Fethiye is established on Telmessos, which is an ancient Lycia city. Name of Telmessos is seen firstly in B.C. 5th Century in the ancient sources. After Alexander's Empire is broken into pieces, city is ruled by Ptolemaioses in B.C. 323 and enters under the rule of Kingdom of Pergamos in B.C. 189. It is located within Asian State of Roman Empire in B.C. 133. City, which is called Anastasiopolis in A.D. 7th Century, is included into Ottoman lands during the reign of Sultan II. Murat in 1424. City, which is called Megri for long period, is named as Fethiye in 1934. Roman Theatre for 5000 people, unearthed from Telmessos ancient city, through excavations, belongs to A.D. 2nd Century. Castle behind the city is surrounded with Middle Age walls. The most interest one of Lycia type rock tombs, located in the rocks above the city, is the one, which belongs to Amyntas, and dates back B.C. 4th Century. Furthermore, Kadyanda, Tlos, Pınara, Sdyma, Letoon, Ksanthos and Patara ancient cities and Saklıkent Canyon; and Kayaköy (Karmilassos), which is an old Greek village around Fethiye, are among the places, required to be visited. Fethiye, having rich historical and natural beauties, unique coves and beaches, becomes the tourism center of the region in the recent years because it has many rest facilities and also it is close to Dalaman Air port. Ölü Deniz (Tranquil Sea-Blue Lagoon), which is a piece from paradise with its tranquil sea, a long beach and surrounding forests, is the rest area in 17 km far from Fethiye. Moreover, city becomes focus of interest of parascenders due to paragliding flies, made in the recent years in Baba Mount in Fethiye.

APHRODISIAS

Aphrodisias ancient city is located in Aydın Province, Karacasu County, Geyre village. Findings, obtained from excavations, which are made on the hill, on which theatre leans and called acropolis, show that first settlement here dates back Early Bronze Age, B.C. 2800-2200 years. Ancient sources provide very little information about the city. City was called Ninoe according to Stephanos from Byzantium. It is started to use Aphrodisias name by beginning from Hellenistic period. Name of Aphrodisias appears on coined silver and bronze coins, minted at the end of B.C. 2nd Century. City is not only an important religious center but also reaches top point with high level of welfare and becomes famous with developments in the scope of art, literature and idea in Roman period. Although bishopric is settled in the city with Christianity, as Aphrodite cult is very common here, paganism survives in Aphrodisias for long period. After city is called Stavropolis, paganism ends in the city. Anatolian Seljuks dominate the region in 11th and 13th Century. Aphrodisias is the city of Caria Region. It is accepted that name of Geyre village, established between Aphrodisias ruins, is originated from Caria. Geyre village in Aphrodisias site, is moved into 1 km. west of the city after the earthquake in 1956. The first excavations in Aphrodisias are made by a French man, Paul Gaudin, in 1904-1905 years, and then excavations are made by Italian Giulio Jacopi in 1937. Essential great excavations in Aphrodisias are started by Prof. Dr. Kenen T. Erim in 1961. He unearths "Sculpturing school" here. Works of sculptors from Aphrodisias, making sculptures by processing the marbles, obtained from the marble quarries, containing white, blue and gray colored marble in 2 km east of the city, are exported to Mediterranean World. Furthermore, famous men of science, literature and idea such as physician Xenocrates, man of letters Chariton and philosopher Alexsander grow up in the city. Works, unearthed from Aphrodisias excavations, are exhibited in the Museum within the site. Aphrodisias is the city of beauty goddess Aphrodite.

Fethiye

Hidden City-Fethiye

Temple of Aphrodite in Aphrodisias is constructed according to Ion order in B.C. 1st Century. Temple with 13 erected columns is turned into a Christian basilica in A.D. 5th Century. Tetrapylon structure, belonging to period of Emperor Hadrian, is restored and erected. Odeon, which is protected well, is constructed in A.D. 2nd Century. Bishop Palace is the structure of A.D. 5th Century. Porches in the north of Agora are in the dor order and porch in the south is in Ion order and is known as Tiberius Porch due to its construction period. Monumental Roman Baths are constructed during the period of emperor Hadrian (117-138). Pool and basilica building are located in the south of Agora. Theatre, which is constructed in Late Hellenistic period and repaired during the reign of emperor Marcus Aurelius (161-180) in Roman period, has a capacity for 10 000 people. Theatre Baths are located in the south of theatre. Agora gate complex is situated in the north of theatre. Stadium structure, which is protected in the best manner in Ancient age, is in the sizes of 262 m. X 59 m. and it is constructed in A.D. 1st Century and has a capacity for 30 000 people. Sebasteion structure belonging to A.D. 1st Century, is constructed with three floors and Dor column headers are used in the first floor and Ion column headers are used in the second floor and Corinthian column headers are used in the third floor. Sebasteion structure, which is a temple, in which it is worshipped to the emperor, is decorated with marble reliefs and sculptures, containing emperor and mythological scenes. Sebasteion is derived from "Sebastos" word, which is Greek translation of "Augustus" word in Latin language. Sebastos word means "merciful, proud and great" in Helen language.

Views from Afrodisiyas

Historical Theater - Aphrodisiyas

Views from Afrodisiyas

Travertines-Pamukkale

HIERAPOLIS / PAMUKKALE

Hierapolis ancient city, located in 20 km far from Denizli, is established by Pergamon King II. Eumenes (B.C. 197-159). It is included into Roman Empire with will of Pergamon King III. Attalos in B.C. 133. Although name of Hierapolis means "Sacred City", it is also supposed that city is called Hierapolis due to Hiera, wife of Telephos, who is the legendary founder of Bergama. Ancient city is intimate to natural wonder Pamukkale, which is "white paradise", arising from south slope of Çal Mount and constituted by the nature with accumulation of waters, containing calcium oxide. Hierapolis is also first degree archaeological and natural site area, which is required to

Historical Theater - Pamukkale

be protected, with its such position, at the same time. As it is believed that hot water sources here have the healing feature for some diseases, it becomes an important cult and a settlement center in the ancient age. It has an important position with its thermal springs in these days. City often witnesses earthquake events and is toppled substantially by the earthquake, occurred in the period of emperor Tiberius (14-37), in A.D. 17. Reestablished city is developed very much in A.D. 2nd and 3rd Century. As there are many Jewish people in the city, it affects Christianity promulgation here quickly. Philip the Apostle is killed here in A.D. 80. Hierapolis becomes the bishopric center in the Christianity period. Also, a great church is constructed for the name of Philip the Apostle. First excavations are made in Hierapolis for short period by German teams at the end of 19th Century. Hierapolis excavations are carried out by Italian archaeologists since 1957. The most magnificent opus of Hierapolis ancient city is its theatre, which is protected well. Theatre stage, which is constructed in A.D. 2nd Century, is decorated with reliefs, containing mythological subjects. Reliefs, depicting Dionysus regiment, are exhibited in the museum. Theatre is restored in 3rd Century. Roman baths, which are protected quite well, are constructed in A.D. 2nd Century and its one section is repaired and serves as Museum building in these days and also works, unearthed from the excavations, are exhibited here. Extant remains of Temple of Apollo, which is constructed in Late Hellenistic period, belong to A.D. 3rd Century. God Apollo is head god of the city. A monumental fountain structure, dated back A.D. 3rd Century, is located in front of the temple. Moreover, there is a cave, called Plutonium and emitting poisonous gases, near the temple. Christianity basilica, composed of three naves, is constructed in A.D. 6th Century. St. Philip Martyrium, located in the east of city, belongs to 5th Century and is an octagonal structure in the sizes of 20 x 20m. There is a main avenue, dividing the city at northern-southern direction. Byzantine Gate and Gate of Domitian, constructed by the order of Julius Frontinus, who is Western Anatolian Council of Roman Empire in A.D. 82-83 years, are located on this avenue. The colonnaded street here belongs to the period of emperor Domitianus (A.D.81-96). The structure, which is called northern baths, must have been constructed at the end of A.D. 2nd Century and at the beginning of 3rd Century. This structure is turned into the church in A.D. 5th Century. Necropolis, located in the north of city, has the greatest and best protected necropolis area among ancient cities in Anatolia. Tumulus, sarcophagus and house type tombs are located in necropolis, developing from Late Hellenistic period to Early Christianity period.

XANTHUS/ Kınık

It is one of the most important cities of Lycia Region. Its name is derived from Xanthus Stream, which is the old name of Esen Stream. We know Xanthus due to their

Pamukkale

Ksanthos

war against Persians in B.C. 545 for the first time in the history. They do not surrender and they disappear by combating. Moreover, we learn from Epopee of Iliad by Homer that Xanthus People participate into Trojan Wars in B.C. 1200. After Alexander the Great finishes Persian rule in Anatolia, city enters under rule of Macedonia Empire in B.C. 133 and is ruled by Ptolemaioses in B.C. 309 and enters under Roman rule in B.C. 42. It becomes a bishopric center in Byzantine age. After Arabian invasions in A.D. 7th Century, city is abandoned completely. First inspections are made in the city, having the most interesting remains of ancient age, by English Charles Fellows in 1838 and he takes away some detected reliefs and architectural pieces to London. Excavations in Xanthus are carried out by French scientists since 1950.

We can list old structure remains in Xanthus ancient city as follows: Theatre, constructed in Roman period, is protected well. Agora of city also belongs to Roman age and must have been constructed in A.D. 2nd or 3rd century. City Gate, constructed in Hellenistic Period, Vespasian Gate, constructed in A.D. 69-79 years and called with the name of Roman emperor and Byzantine church are some of the remains, located in the ancient city. Reliefs of Nereidler Monument, belonging to B.C. 400 year and whose foundations remain, reliefs of Harpi Monument belonging to B.C. 480-470 years and also reliefs of Tomb with Lion, belonging to B.C. 550-540 year and Payava Monument, belonging to B.C. 4th Century, are carried to British Museum completely in 19th Century. Tower Tomb, located in Roman acropolis and belonging to B.C. 4th Century, is protected well. Reliefs of Tower with Epigraph monument and reliefs on Lycia Tower Tomb, dated back B.C. 4th Century are protected in Istanbul Archeological Museum. Furthermore, there are many tomb monuments and remains in the ancient city.

LETOON / Bozoluk

Letoon city is established for the name of Leto, who becomes pregnant from god Zeus and mother of god Apollo and Artemis. This city is the sacred place of Lycia Union and it is in 4 km. far from Xanthus city. The oldest settlement traces in the city date back B.C. 7th Century. Remains and captured epigraphs show that here is a religious and political area. Excavations in Letoon ancient city, beginning in 1950,

Letoon

are carried out by French scientists. There are three temples side by side in the sanctuary in the site center. Temple, constructed in Ion order in the most western side and dated as B.C. 3rd Century, is consecrated to Leto; small temple, located in the middle, belongs to B.C. 4th Century and is consecrated to goddess Artemis and; temple in the east is constructed according to Dor order in Hellenistic period and is consecrated to Apollo. Nymphaion, constructed during the period of Emperor Hadrian (A.D.117-138); and monastery, dated as A.D. 4th Century and small exedra, belonging to Hellenistic period, are located in southern-west of the temples. There are remains of Hellenistic and Roman period porches, constructed in Ion and Dor order in the north of temples. Theatre structure, which is placed on a hillside, is constructed in the Hellenistic period. Letoon is abandoned in A.D. 7th Century.

PATARA / Gelemiş

Patara is an important Lycia city and also it becomes capital city of Lycia Union. It is one of six cities of Lycia Union, having three voting rights. Cities, located in Lycia Union, are used to organize their meetings in the council building of union in Patara. Patara, which is also an important port city, is known as Patar in Hittite language; it is known as Pattara in Lycia language. Findings, obtained from excavations, which are made in the city, show that settlements here date back B.C. 8th Century. City is known as prophecy center of Apollo, fulfilling prophecy function only in the winter. Furthermore, it is said that god Apollo was born in Patara. Patara is also a very important city in Roman period and becomes capital city of Lycia-Pamphilia states. Patara port has importance in terms of cereal warehouse and its shipment. One of 3 cereal warehouses, located in Eastern Mediterranean Region in Roman period, is located in (Granarium) Patara. City, which also maintains its development in Byzantine period, is consecrated by Christian people. St. Nicholaos, who is known as "Father Christmas", is from Patara. As Patara port starts to fill with sand in the course of time and boats have difficulty in approaching, Patara losses its importance. It attracts attention that great part of remains to be seen in the city, are under the sand today. Gate with three eyes, which is protected well in the entrance of city, is constructed in A.D. 100. According to the epigraph on it, there were busts of people, belonging to family of Lycia's Roman Governor Mettius Modestus on six cantilevers in two sides of the gate. After it is passed through this gate, there are Roman baths, Christianity period basilica and Vespasianus (A.D. 69-79) baths. Theatre, which is cov-

Patara

Kaş

ered by sands partially, belongs to middle of A.D. 2nd Century. Known biggest assembly building of ancient period in Anatolia is located in the north of theatre. Lighthouse Remains are situated in the west of city. Cereal warehouse, which is called Gargarium (silo) and belongs to period of emperor Hadrian (118-137), reaches today in a very well protected position, in the west of port, which is march in these days. Furthermore, Byzantine Church, Port Bath, Marciana Tomb, temple remains, Port Basilica, agora remains are some of the old structure remains in the ancient city. Excavations in Patara ancient city is carried out by Prof. Dr. Fahri Işık from Akdeniz University.

KAŞ / ANTIPHELLOS

It is understood certainly from a bilingual epigraph, which is found in Kaş, that city under Kaş is Antiphellos. However, the older name of Kaş is Habesos. Antiphellos is a very small settlement place in B.C. IV. Century and Phellos, which is located slightly above it, is the port of city. However, while entering into Hellenistic period, Phellos goes down, Antiphellos develops and comes into prominence more. This case also continues in Roman period, city is developed owing to trade of cedar, obtained from regional forests, and sponge fishing, and it gets rid of being port of Phellos and becomes a self sufficient and rich city. Wall remains belonging to Hellenistic period are seen in good order in Meis Island's frontage of the altitude, described as acropolis. However, northern and western directions of such wall remains do not reach today. Wall remains in the seaside can be seen today. There are 24 women figures in the frieze part of a house type tomb chamber, which is protected well and belongs to B.C. 4th Century in the west of city. Seafront theatre of Antiphellos ancient city, in the right of road, going to Çukurbağ Peninsula, located in the western part of the city, is in quite good condition. The most famous monument of Kaş is a sarcophagus formed from a single block on Uzun Çarşı Avenue among the rug shops. As script in Lycia language with eight lines on the sarcophagus, which belongs to B.C. 4th Century and reaches today in a good condition, can not be read, it is known whom it belongs to. However, such sarcophagus is called "Sarcophagus of King" publicly.

KEKOVA

As settlement areas are submerged due to sinkings, occurred as a result of earthquakes in the region, sunken cities and islands are constituted. The biggest one of these islands is Kekova Island. This region is generally called Kekova due to this island. There are a Byzantine church and remains belonging to various periods in Kekova Island and remains of sunken buildings in coasts of the island. Ucagiz village (Theimussa) and Kalekoy (Simena) settlement areas are located in Anatolian Side of Kekova Island. Moreover, sunken areas are located in the coasts of Theimussa and Simena ancient settlements and also, a Middle Age Castle, Roman Bath, a small Theatre and Necropolis and the other remains are located in Simena ancient city.

Kekova

DEMRE

Church, which is called Saint Nicholas Church, is in Demre. Saint Nicholas carries out his bishopric service in this church, which was existing in advance. When Saint Nicholas, who increased to the sainthood level in Christian world, was died, his funeral was buried into a sarcophagus, belonging to Late Roman period and placed into a middle abscissa in the south direction of this church. The church is a basilical structure with three abscissas, two narthexes and a courtyard. It is extended in 6th Century. Church is damaged substantially during Arabian invasions and robberies in 7th-9th Centuries. It is repaired by the order of emperor Constantine Monomachos (1042-1055) and his wife Zoe and surrounded with a wall in 11th Century. Sarcophagus of Saint Nicholas is broken and robbed by Italian merchants and his bones are received and carried to Bari city in Italy in 1087. The church undergoes repair in 19th and 20th Centuries. It becomes famous due to its connection with Father Christmas since 1950.

MYRA

Myra ancient city is located immediately in the north of Demre. There are many rock tombs, belonging to B.C. 4th Century, caved in rocks in various type and affecting and fascinating the human and a Roman period theatre, which is protected very well, here. Also, Andriake city, which is the port of Myra, is located at the area in which Demre stream flows into the sea. There is also Granarium (cereal warehouse) structure, which is an important structure of Roman Age and constructed in the period of Emperor Hadrianus (117-138), here. Myra becomes an important city owing to this port city, which departure point of big cereal ships, supplying food for Roma.

Demre

Myra (At Next)

Olympus

OLYMPOS

Olympus ancient city, located in Lycia Region, is a port city, established in Hellenistic period. Name of city appears on the coins, minted in B.C. 2nd Century. City, which is established within greeneries and in the mouth of a river, reaching to the sea, survives in Hellenistic, Roman, Byzantine, partially Ottoman periods, city losses its importance and is abandoned completely in 15th Century. Ancient city has acropolis, constructed in Middle Age on a small hill and surrounded with walls. The bridge, which combines two sides on the river, house of Bishop belonging to 6th Century, Roman period temple, Bath structure, Roman period theatre, Colonnaded street, Byzantine basilica, agora and gymnasium remains, memorial tombs, are some of the old structure remains in the ancient city. Moreover, necropolis of the city is located on the hill at the west of ancient city. It is believed that flame, arising from natural gasses and coming out of the ground continuously in these days in Çiralı'da (Burning Stone) near Olympus city, belongs to monster Chimaira, living here and spitting fire from breath. Further more, as it is believed that it is a place, belonging to god of forgers Hefaistos, here is accepted as a sacred place. Ancient sources inform that there is a temple here. Availability of a church remains here, indicates that here is known as a sacred place and worshipped in the Christianity period.

Çıralı

Theater-Phaselis

PHASELIS / Tekirova

Establishment of Phaselis ancient city, located in Tekirova village, dates back beginning of B.C. 6th Century. City is established on a peninsula as Rhodes colony. It is a city, located between greeneries and having three ports. City gets rich owing to marine trade and develops very much. City enters under rule of respectively Persia, Alexander the Great, Ptolemaios, Roman, Byzantine and it becomes bishopric center in A.D. 6th Century in the Christianity period. As Alanya and Antalya ports come into prominence in Anatolian Seljuk Empire period, Phaselis losses its importance and abandoned in 12th Century. Aqueducts belonging to Roman age, is located in the entrance of city. Important structure remains in ancient city are located in two sides of large avenue, which connects the military port in the north and commercial port in the south. We can list remains of these structures as follows. By beginning from south port, Late Period agora and Domitian (A.D. 69-79) agora, Hadrian (117-138) agora, Byzantine period basilica, Bath, gymnasium and fountain structures are located in the west of avenue; Hadrian Gate, city square, bath, toilet, belonging to A.D. 3rd-4th Centuries; and Roman theatre, constructed in A.D. 2nd Century onto the theatre, constructed according to Hellenistic tradition in the hillside of acropolis and walls surrounding acropolis are located. Ancient sources inform that there is Athena temple mainly in acropolis within the city and there are other temples in the city. Moreover, necropolis areas are located out of the city.

Phaselis

Grooved Minaret, Watch Tower -Antalya

ANTALYA

Attaleia, which is a port city, is established between B.C. 159-138 by Pergamon king II. Attalos. City is named as Attaleia due to the name of its founder. City, entering under Roman Rule in B.C. 133, becomes bishopric center in A.D. 5th Century. City, entering under Anatolian Seljuk Empire Rule in 1207, is included into Ottoman lands in 1426. Antalya, which is a small city until the recent times, becomes one of the most important tourism centers today due to tourism, developing in the recent years. Hadrian Gate, constructed in A.D. 130 and with two floors in original within the city, and also Hıdırlık Tower belonging to A.D. 2nd century, Kesik Minare (Broken Minaret) Mosque, which is a Roman temple in advance and turned into the church in Byzantine period and then turned into the mosque in 13th century, within the castle, Fluted Minaret, belonging to period of I. Alaattin Keykubat (1219-1236), 1250 dated Karatay Madrasah, 1570 dated Murat Pasha Mosque and walls surrounding port are among important historical structures in Antalya. Antalya Museum is a museum, which is required to be visited and in which rich archaeological and ethnographic works are exhibited. Kaleiçi region and Düden and Kurşunlu Waterfalls, Saklıkent, in which winter sports are played, and ancient city ruins such as Termessos, Aspendos, Perge, Side, Selge and Köprülü Canyon are the important places, which are required to be visited.

TERMESSOS

Termessos ancient city is established on a natural platform on the top of Güllük Mount in 30 kilometers northernwest of Antalya. It is covered under the scope of Termessos National Park, bearing the name of ancient city, due to the natural and historical richness. Termessos city is established by Solymnians, coming inside Anatolia.

Termessos

Termessians state themselves as Solymnians, one of the native population of Pamphilia in the epigraphs. Their language is seen as a dialect of Pisidia. Although name of city passes in Epopee of Iliad in the context of Bellerophon story for the first time, Termessos comes into existence after Alexander the Great comes to Anatolia in B.C. 334. They live in abundance in Hellenistic and Roman Ages. Termessos peoples are accepted as friendly and allied nation of Roman peoples by Roman Senate and right to regulate their own laws is given to Termessians. The theatre building, which is one of the best protected structures in the ancient city, is constructed in Hellenistic period and stage building is constructed in Roman period in A.D. 2nd Century and has a capacity for 4200 people. Agora of city is ruined very much. Western stoa of the agora, called Attalos stoa, is constructed in Dor order and with two floors and belongs to period of Pergamon king II. Attalos (159-138). Northern stoa is constructed by Osbaras in A.D. I. Century. The best protected structure of the city is Bouleuterion structure, which is constructed in Hellenistic period. Furthermore, Zeus Solymeus Temple, Temple of Artemis dated in Roman Age and also Termessos' main temple, which is constructed in Dor order between 138-192 in Roman age and likely to belong goddess Artemis, Great and Small Temples, which are constructed in the Corinthian order, House of the Founder of the City, Gymnasium, colonnaded street, Hadrian Propylon, cisterns are some of other structure remains in the city. Moreover, tombs caved in rocks, located in north, south and west of the city, cemeteries which are constructed in the form of temple and contain sarcophaguses, are also important and effective feature of Termessos ancient city.

PERGE

It is one of the best protected ancient cities of Turkey. Name of Perge passes as Parha in a bronze tablet, which is captured in the excavations, made on Bogazkoy, which is the capital city of Hittites. Therefore, it indicates that Perge is also known in Hittite period. It is stated in the epigraph on the sculpture base, which is detected in the place, where oldest entrance gate of the city is located, that Perge is established by Kalchas and Mopsos in B.C. 12th Century after Trojan Wars. Perge city comes into existence until Alexander the Great comes in B.C. 333. Perge

Perge

enters under rule of Alexander the Great and then respectively, Ptolemaios in B.C 323, Kingdom of Pergamon in B.C. 190, Roman Empire in B.C. 133. City, beginning to develop in Hellenistic period, makes great progresses. Current excavations in Perge are carried out by Prof. Dr. Haluk Abbasoglu in these days. Works, unearthed from the excavations, are also exhibited in Antalya Museum. The theatre building of the city is Helen-Roman style and is a structure with capacity of 15 000 people. Stage building with two floors, of the theatre, constructed in Roman age, is constructed after A.D. 150. Mythological scenes belonging to god of river Kestros and god of wine Dionysus, are located in the reliefs in stage building. A nymphaion with five niches was located in the exterior surface of stage building. Guard rails, surrounding the orchestra, are made due to the gladiator shows, made in the theatres, in Late Roman period. One of the best protected structures of Perge is the stadium, constructed in A.D. 2nd Century and having capacity for 12 000 people. City Gate is likely to be constructed during the period of Hadrian, an entrance gate is constructed in front of this gate during the period of Septimius Severus and city gate, which is constructed later on, belongs to A.D. 4th Century. Nymphaion and propylon structures, constructed during the period of emperor Septimius Severus (193-211), are located after these structures. Ancient City Gate, having one round tower in both sides, is the oldest structure of Hellenistic period, in Perge. Courtyard with horseshoe style, which is constructed by the order of Plancia Magna, daughter of Bithynia Governor Plancius Varus in 120-122 years, is located after such gate. City wall is constructed in Hellenistic period. Christianity period church with abscissa in the east, agora, which is a small area surrounded with shops and extended in A.D. 4th Century, Roman baths, bishopric basilica, baths, colonnaded street, palaestra, which is constructed in A.D. 41-54 and protected well, Nymphaion, belonging to Hadrianus period and other colonnaded street are the other important structure remains, located in Perge. Acropolis area, located in the north of city, may be the first settlement place in Perge. Necropolis areas are also located at the east and west side of Acropolis.

ASPENDOS

It is an ancient city, located within boundaries of Antalya Province and in the eastern direction. According to ancient sources, Aspendos city is established by colonists from Argos, who come here under the leadership of Mopsos. Aspendos city mints the silver coins for its own name in B.C. 5th Century and becomes member of Maritime Union of Athens. City, entering under Alexander the Great rule in B.C. 334, is ruled by Roma through succession upon death of III. Attalos in B.C. 133. Aspendos city also survives as a rich city in Roman period. All of the remains, located in Aspendos, belong to Roman is leaning on a hill, seats are placed on cradle vaults. Gallery with cloisters, located in the backmost, is added subsequently. Stage building is multistoried and decorated with sculptures. It is stated in Greek and Latin epigraphs, located on the entrance (parados) sections in both sides of stage building that two siblings named as Crispinus and Auspicatus consecrate the theatre in honor of gods of country and emperor family. Theatre undergoes repair substantially. Theatre, which is also open for public visits in these days, becomes the place of social, cultural and artistic activities, opera and ballet festivals from time to time.

Historical Theater-Aspendos

Period and after Roman Period. Theatre building in the city belongs to Roman Empire Age. It is constructed during the period of emperor Marcus Aurelius (161-180) in A.D. 2nd Century. Theatre has a half round plan. Zenon is the architect of the building. This splendid building is the theatre, which reaches today from ancient age and is protected in the best manner. As structure is used as palace in Anatolian Seljuk period, it is protected very well. Theatre has capacity for Fifteen thousand people and although it Besides famous theatre structure in Aspendos ancient city, city gates, agora, basilica (administration building), porch, bouleuterion (city assembly building), nymphaion (fountain), aqueducts, bath, gymnasium, stadium, belonging to Roman Period, are some the old structure remains, located in the ancient city. Necropolis of the city is located at the east side of the acropolis. Moreover, bridge of Anatolian Seljuk period on Köprüçayı, is one of the extant structures in good condition.

Side

SİDE

Side, which an Aeolis Region city, is established by Cymians according to Strabon. Side means "pomegranate" as a word. Pomegranate motif is located on Side coins from B.C. 500 to Roman period. History of city dates back B.C. 7th Century. History of city dates back B.C. 7th Century. After Alexander the Great, city, which enters under rule of respectively Ptoleimaicos between B.C. 301-218 and then Seleucus, is ruled by Roman Empire. Side city has good relations with Roman Empire in B.C. 2nd and 1st Centuries and develops very much. City lives its most prime period during A.D. 2nd and 3rd Centuries. After Roman Empire divides into two pieces in 395, Side city becomes poor adn wall is constructed throughout on the narrowest place of the peninsula in the middle of A.D. 4th Century and half of city is abandoned. Side becomes a bishopric center in 5th and 6th Centuries. Walls, surrounding the city, belong to B.C. 2nd Century. Main Gate, located on the walls, has a good defense feature. Nymphaion, which is City Fountain, is located opposite this gate. Aqueduct is constructed at the end of A.D. 2nd

Side

Century and repaired at the beginning of 3rd Century. Two colonnaded street, opening to the city from main gate, is constructed in A.D. 2nd Century. Agora, surrounded with porches, belongs to A.D. 2nd Century. Temple of Tykhe, dated as A.D. 2nd Century, is located in the middle of Agora; a toilet building, having seat for 24 people, is located in the north of agora. Theatre of the city is constructed in A.D. 2nd Century and orchestra is surrounded with a high guard rail in order to protect audiences from gladiator plays and wild animal fightings in Late Roman period. According to epigraphs, theatre is turned into an outdoor church in 5th and 6th Centuries. Baths near Agora are constructed in A.D. 5th Century. Restored baths serve as Side Museum today. A monumental entrance and three fountains were located between square in front of this bath and western side of agora. Monumental Gate provided the passage into the internal passage in Roman age. Temple of Dionysus, between theatre and colonnaded street, belongs to Roman period. Christianity basilica is protected partially and monumental baths near the port are constructed in A.D. 2nd Century. Temple of Apollo and Temple of Athens, dated as second half of A.D. 2nd Century, are constructed in the Corinthian order. One section of Temple of Apollo is restored and it is erected. Christian basilica, belonging to A.D. 5th Century, is constructed on the foundations of Apollo and Athens Temples, it is seen that a church is constructed inside this basilica in 8th and 9th Century. Temple of Men, constructed in A.D. 3rd Century, Small Byzantine Church, belonging to 8th and 9th Century, and Byzantine basilica, belonging to 5th or 6th Centuries, are some of the other structure remains in Side. Substantial part of the ancient city remains under the modern Side and witnesses great destructions. Side is one of the leading holiday resorts today. Manavgat Waterfall in 5 km. far from Side and also Seleukeia ancient city, in the vicinity of Şıhlar Village, bounded to Manavgat, are the places, which are required to be visited.

Alanya

ALANYA

County, located along Mediterranean Sea, develops substantially owing to the tourism. Its name in ancient age is "Korakesion" and city is established by pirates on a rocky hill which dominates the land and the sea, in B.C. 2nd Century and used as a base for the slave trade. It enters under Roman rule in A.D. 65. City, remaining within boundaries of Eastern Roman Empire in 395, is captured by Anatolian Seljuk Sultan I. Alaeddin Keykubat in 1220 and city is called "Alaiye". Castles, composed of three sections as external, middle and internal, are surrounded with strong walls. Remains of palace, military buildings, cisterns, remains of church, Akşebe Sultan Mosque and Tomb, constructed in 1230, Süleymaniye Mosque, bazaar and hostelry structures are located on the castle. Alaiye is also a summer capital city of Anatolian Seljuk Empire at the same time. Red Tower (1226), constructed for defense purpose, and shipyard (1227) structure are located along the sea. Alaiye city is the naval base of Anatolian Seljuks in Mediterranean Sea. Damlataş Cave and Archeological Museum in Alanya, which is a holiday town, and Dim Caves in the vicinity of county are the places, which are must see places.

Damlataş Cave Alanya

Anamur

ANAMUR / ANEMURIUM

Anamur is a holiday town and its name in ancient age is Anemurium. Ancient city is located a highland of Cilicia Region. Name of the city passes in the ancient sources in B.C. 4th Century for the first time. City develops substantially in Roman period. It is exposed to Arabian invasions in 7th Century, Turks come and settle here by beginning from 11th Century and they dominate the region. Remains of theater, palestra, Odeon, basilica, baths and other buildings are located in Anemurium ancient city. Works, unearthed from excavations, made on the ancient city, are exhibited in Anamur Museum. A castle, which is protected very well, is located in the seaside in 8 km. east of Anamur. Castle, constructed by Romans in A.D. 3rd Century probably, is repaired during the reign of Karamanoğlu I. İbrahim Bey in 14th Century and also a mosque is constructed inside it. Castle, which is in a very good condition at the end of repair, is called Mamure Castle.

SİLİFKE / SELEUCEIA

Silifke county, located along Göksu River, is in 8 km. far from the sea. However, it makes important progresses in tourism in the recent years. Silifke is located on the ancient city. The ancient city is established by I. Seleucus at the beginning of B.C. 3rd Century and the city is called Seleuceia. City, which is included into territories of Roman Empire in B.C. 67, lives its most prime period in A.D. 2nd and 3rd Centuries. City, which is exposed to Arabian invasions in 7th Century, witnesses 3rd Crusade in 12th Century. Silifke enters under the rule of respectively Anatolian Seljuks Empire at the beginning of 13th Century and Karamanoğulları and then Ottomans in 1471. Silifke Castle is located in the immediately vicinity of the city. Castle, which is used in Hellenistic and Roman periods, is repaired subsequently and becomes a Castle of The Middle Ages. There are various structure remains within the castle. Cistern, which is called Tekir Warehouse, is located in the east of castle. Remains of ancient theatre building are located in the east of cistern. Roman Temple, which is located within the city and whose single column reaches today, is constructed in the Corinthian order in A.D. 2nd Century. Roman Bridge, which is constructed on Göksu River in A.D. 77-78 years, is destroyed until its foundations except three eyes in the north, and constructed again in

Uzuncaburç

1875. Ave Thekla Church, dated as A.D. 5th Century, is located in 1 km. south of Silifke. Alahan Monastery, located in 22 km north of Mut county, bounded to Mersin province, must have been constructed in the middle of 5th and 6th Centuries. Monastery, which is constructed in front of the cave, is a community of structures, composed of Eastern Church, Western Church, Cave Church, Baptistery, Hamam, Cemetery and the other monastery structures.

UZUNCABURÇ / OLBA DİOCAESAREA

Olba ruins, located in Uzuncaburc in 25 km. north of Silifke, is protected very well. Zeus Olbios Temple was situated here in Hellenistic Period. City is called "Diocaesarea" during the period of Empire Vespasian (A.D. 69-79) in Roman period. We can list the structure remains, located in the city, as follows. Zeus Olbios Temple, which is constructed in the Corinthian order during the period of I. Seleucus in B.C. 3rd Century, is turned into the church in the early Christianity period. Temple, which is called Tychaion and presented to Good Luck Goddess, is constructed in the Corinthian order and belongs to A.D. 2nd Century. Colonnaded streets within the city belong to Roman Age. Theatre building is constructed in B.C. 3rd Century. Gate with three eyes, opening to north of city, belongs to A.D. 1st Century and "Diocaesarea" script is available in its epigraph.

KORYKION ANTRON / KORYKOS

Korykos ancient city, located in 15 km. east of Silifke, is known as Cennet Cehennem (Korykion Antron) in the region. Highway is passing inside Korykos city. There is a castle, constructed in A.D. 2nd Century, in the seaside. Castle undergoes repair during the reign of Karamanogullari in the first half of 15th Century. There are a church, cistern and building remains in the castle. The other castle is Maiden's Castle, which is located on an island in 200 m. off shore and surrounded with walls, which are fortified with eight towers and constructed for military purpose. Castle undergoes repair during the reign of Karamanoğlu II. Ibrahim Bey in 1448. There is a small church and cistern within Maiden's Castle. Both castles are bounded to each other with a wall inside the sea at that period. Two deep fosses, located in the city, established in the

Mamuriye Castle

Maiden Castle

Views from Heaven and Hell Caves

north of highway, are called Cennet and Cehennem. There is Church of The Virgin Mary, constructed in A.D. 5th Century and surrounded with wall, in the great foss, called Cennet. As rise and fall of second foss, located in the north of such great foss, is very difficult and it is risen and fallen by stairs, it is called Cehennem. Remains in Korykos ancient city belong to Roman Period and after Roman Period. Walls, surrounding Korykos city, belong to A.D. 1st Century. Building remains such as temple, basilica, monastery church, cathedral and rock tombs and necropolis areas are located in the city.

TARSUS / TARSOS

Findings, obtained from the archeological excavations, made in Gözlükule in the southern-east of Tarsus, show that first settlement here dates back Neolithic age. Region is ruled respectively by Hittites by beginning from B.C. 1500, Assyrians in B.C. 1200, Persians in B.C. 546. City enters under the rule of respectively Alexander the Great in B.C. 333, Seleucians after B.C. 323, Cilicia Region is bounded to Roman Empire in B.C. 66, Tarsos also becomes the center of state. Marcus Antonius and Egyptian Queen Cleopatra meet here in B.C. 41. City lives the most prime period in Roman Age. After Roman Empire is divided into two pieces in 395, city maintains its importance. It is exposed to Arabian invasions in 7th Century. City is captured by Seljuks some

Views from Heaven and Hell Caves

Tarsus

The Cave of the Seven Sleepers

time at the end of 11th Century, however, city is ruled by Crusaders in 1097. Then, city enters under the rule of respectively Byzantines, Armenians, Memluks and finally Ottomans in 1516. Name of city in the ancient age is Tarsos. Name of Tarsos passes in the sources in B.C. 5th Century for the first time. Name of Tarsus is originated from Tarsos. Furthermore, Saint Paulus, who is one of Jesus's Apostles and plays an important role for the propagation of Christianity, is from Tarsus. Cleopatra Gate, which is the western entrance gate of the city, and constructed in A.D. 2nd Century and renewed in 6th Century, Pit of Saint Paul, Saint Paul Church, reconstructed in 1862, remains of Roman Temple and Roman Bath, constructed in A.D. 2nd Century, Old Mosque, called Church Mosque, which is constructed as Saint Paul Church in 1102 and turned into the mosque in 1415, Kubat Paşa Madrasah, constructed in 1550, and also Ulu Mosque, Kırkkaşık Bazaar, restored Tarsus Houses under protection, Tarsus Waterfall, flowing over ancient period tombs, Tarsus Museum and Ancient Road, belonging to B.C. 1st Century and Seven Sleepers Cave, in 14 km. far from Tarsus are the places, which are required to be visited.

Adana

ADANA

Adana, which is fourth greatest city of Turkey, is established in two sides of Seyhan River, irrigating fertilized Çukurova lands. First settlement started in Adana region since Neolithic period. Region enters under the rule of Hittites and then respectively Assyrians, Urartians, Babylonians and then Persians. Alexander the Great finishes Persian rule in B.C. 333, after his death in B.C. 323, region enters under the rule of respectively Seleuceians and Ptolemaioses and then Roman Empire in B.C. 1st Century. City, exposed to Arabian invasions in B.C. 7th Century, witnesses Crusades in 11th Century. Region is ruled by respectively Seljuks, Cilicia Armenians, Memluks and Ramazanoğulları. It is included into Ottoman territories in 1517. The oldest opus in Adana belongs to Roman period on Seyhan River and it is Stone Bridge with 21 eyes, which is constructed during the period of emperor Hadrian (117-138), repaired during the period of emperor Iustinianos I (527-565) in 6th Century. Ağaca Mosque is constructed in 1409. Ulu Mosque is built during the period of Ramazanoğulları between 1513-1541. There are tomb, having sarcophagus with three tiles inside, and madrasah, constructed in 1540, and also bath, bazaar and palace buildings around the mosque. Yağ Mosque, called Old Mosque, which is turned into mosque from an old church in 1501, 1541 dated Hasan Kethüda Mosque, 1530 dated Bazaar Bath, Covered Bazaar, Clock Tower, constructed between 1879-1882, are some of the other old structures in Adana. Adana Archeological Museum, which is rich in terms of archaeological works, ethnography Museum, which is turned into a museum in 1983, from the church, constructed in 1845, Suphi Pasha Residence, organized as Ataturk Museum are the important places, which are required to be visited. Moreover, there are so many castles and sites around Adana. Karatepe Outdoor Museum/Site is located in 130 km northern-east of Adana in the vicinity of Kadirli county. Remains of summer palace of king Asitavata, belonging to Late Hittite period dated as B.C. 700, are located here. As there are bilingual script as Hittite hieroglyphics and Phoenician on an orthostatic epigraph near stone reliefs (orthostatic), containing various scenes, it facilitates solution of Hittite hieroglyphics. Misis Mosaic Museum, containing mosaics of Early Byzantine period, is located in Misis in 27 km east of Adana. Also, Anavarza ancient city and castle is located on Ceyhan/Kadirli road in 20 km. east of Adana. Anavarza Castle is located on a steep hill in the place where bottom land ends, in the northern-east of Çukurova, containing fertile lands. There are ancient Anavarza city remains in the lowland. Although Anazarba, Aynzarba and Anazarbus names pass in the sources, name of Anazarva is used in these days. History of city dates back B.C. 1st Century. City enters under Roman rule during the period of Emperor Claudius (A.D. 41-54). Great public works are made in the city; city develops and gets rich in Roman age. City is toppled by the earthquakes, occurred during the period of Emperor Iustinos (518-527) and Iustinianos I (527-565) and it is constructed again. City, which is exposed to Arabian invasions in 6th and 7th centuries, is captured finally and becomes an Arabic city, named as Ain Zorba. Then even though it is ruled by respectively Eastern Roman (Byzantine), Cilicia Armenians, Mongols and Memluks and captured by Cilicia Armenians again in 1375, city could not return its old lively life and it is abandoned. Afterwards, region enters under Ottomans rule. Dilekkaya Village is located in these days on Anavarza ruins, spread into a large area. Ancient city was surrounded with walls. The city had four main gates. The walls were fortified with 56 towers. Although scientific excavations are not started in the ancient city, rich base mosaics are unearthed during the foundation excavations.

ANTAKYA / ANTIOKHEIA

After death of Alexander the Great in A.D. 323, his established empire begins to break into pieces. Syria is controlled by Seleucus Dynasty (B.C. 312-B.C. 65). Seleucus I names the city, which he established along Asi River in B.C. 301, as Antiocheia, due to the name of his son Anatiokhos I (B.C. 280-261). City is the capital city of Syria Seleuceians, when it is controlled by Romans in B.C. 65, city becomes the capital city of Syria State. City lives its prime period in Roman period, population of the city reaches up to 150 000. City also maintains its importance in Christianity period and becomes control center and religious capital city of Eastern Bishopric. City is toppled by the terrible earthquake, occurred in 526. City, which enters under the rule of respectively Arabians in 638, Byzantines in 965, Anatolian Seljuks in 1084, is captured by Crusaders in 1097 and bounded to Kingdom of Jerusalem. City, which is captured by Memluks in 1268, is included into Ottoman territories during the period of Yavuz Sultan Selim in 1515 finally. Antakya is an important city in terms of Christianity history. Although Christianity religion begins in Jerusalem, it is propagated to Syria, Anatolia and Middle East via Antakya. St. Petros, one of Jesus' Apostles, establishes a communion in St. Petros Cave in Antakya in A.D. 29 and they make first worshipping here and they are called first Christians". This cave is turned into a church in 13th Century. After Pope VI. Paul visits this church in 1963, here is turned into a pilgrimage place for Christians. It is an important visitation place in these days. Old Antakya Castle and walls, surrounding the city, are constructed during the period of Seleucus I in B.C. 3rd Century. There were Gates, called St. Paul,

St. George, Bridge, Duke and Dog, in the city walls surrounded ancient city. Remains of aqueducts, belonging to emperor Traianus period (98-117), in Bagriyanik district, are known as "Memikli Bridge" with its current name. Current Military College, which is called Daphne and in which Roman soldier and civil rich people reside in Roman period, is one of the rare places, which are required to be visited. As it is said that mythological tale between Water Sprite "Daphne" and god Apollo occurs here, here is called with this name. Furthermore, as there is a military post here in Roman Age, it is said that here is called "Military College". Habib Neccar Mosque, which is turned from church to mosque, Ulu Mosque from Memluk period, Old Antakya Houses are also among the important architectural works in the city. However, the most important place, which is required to be visited in Antakya, is Antakya Archeological Museum, in which the richest mosaics of the world are exhibited. Seleuceia Pieria ancient city, which is located in 8 km. north of the place where Asi River flows into Mediterranean Sea, within boundaries of Samandagi county, is established by Seleucus I. (B.C. 312-280). Capital city was the port city of Antiokheia. The most important structure here is Titus Tunnel, which is constructed in order to protect the port of city from floodwaters. An epigraph, containing names of Emperor Vespasian (A.D. 69-79) and his son Titus (A.D. 79-81), is located on the rock in the tunnel. Moreover, rock tombs in Beşikli Cave, are the worth seeing places.

Views from Antakya Museum

Anıtkabir (Mausoleum) - Ankara

ANKARA

Findings, obtained from excavations, which are made in Ankara and in the surrounding , show that settlements here date back prehistoric ages. Although there are small scaled settlements belonging to Hittite period (B.C. 1600-1200) in the vicinity of city, important settlements are appeared in Phrygia period (B.C. 750-300). It is seen that city is ruled by respectively Galats in B.C. 3rd Century and Roman Empire in B.C. 25. City develops substantially in Roman period. After Roman Empire is divided into two pieces in 395, Ankara remains in Eastern Roman territories. While city is ruled by Anatolian Seljuks in 1147, city is included into Ottoman territories in 1360. City, which is captured by Timur in 1402, enters under Ottomans rule certainly during the reign of Çelebi Mehmet in 1411. Ankara becomes capital city of Republic of Turkey in 1923. Name of Ankara is derived from "Ancyra", which is its first name in the history and means ship anchor. Afterwards, this name changes as "Angora", and then Ankara finally.

One of the most important structures in the city is Temple of Augustus, which is also called Ankara Temple (Monumentum Ancyranum). Successes of emperor Augustus (B.C.27-A.D.14) are explained in Latin and Greek language on the wall of temple, constructed between B.C. 25-20 years. Temple is modified with some additions in A.D. 2nd Century. Hacı Bayram Mosque is constructed at the beginning of 15th Century at northern-west corner of the temple, which is turned into the church in Christianity period. Roman Baths, belonging to Emperor Caracalla (A.D. 211-217) period, are protected well. Iulianus Column is erected in 362 in order to commemorate passage of Emperor Iulianus (361-363) from Ankara. Alaeddin Mosque, belonging Anatolian Seljuks period, is constructed in Citadel in 1198-1199. Aslanhane Mosque, dated 1290, is constructed in Beylics period. 1565 dated New Mosque, belonging to Ottoman period, Zincirli Mosque, construct during the reign of Fatih Sultan Mehmet, 1427 dated Karacabey Mosque, 1427 dated Hacı Bayram Mosque, Mahmut Paşa Bazaar, constructed between 1464-1471, Kurşunlu Hostelry, constructed at the end of 15th Century, are the important historical structures in the city. Furthermore, Ottoman period houses are seen in Ic Kale, Samanpazarı, Hacı Bayram and Hacı Dogan districts. It is not known when Ankara Castle, rising on a rocky hill, is constructed. However, it is mentioned certainly about availability of a castle here in B.C. 2nd Century. Current castle is composed of two sections as Citadel and Bailey. Castle is extended in Roman, Byzantine and Ottoman periods and undergoes repairs in the various periods. Ankara Castle, which is one of the thought structures when it is mentioned about Ankara, is also one of the important places, which are required to be visited. "The Museum of Anatolian Civilizations", which is constituted as a result of Mahmut Paşa Bazaar and Kurşunlu Hostelry, is one of the richest museums of the world, in which works of paleolithic, neolithic, chalcolithic, bronze age, iron age, Assyrian Colonies Age, Hittite, Phrygia, Urartu, Late Hittite, Hellenistic, Roman, Byzantine, Seljuks and Ottoman periods are exhibited. Ethnography Museum, which is constructed between 1925-1930 years, is a rich museum, in which valuable and various ethnographic works are exhibited. Roman Bath-Outdoor Museum, Picture and Sculpture Museum, Independence War Museum, Republic Museum are the other museums, located in the city. Moreover, Anıtkabir /Mausoleum of Mustafa Kemal Ataturk, founder of Republic of Turkey, which is symbol of Ankara and is constructed between 1944-1953 and Anıtkabir Museum are the visitation places of domestic and foreign visitors, coming to Ankara.

GORDION

It is near Yassıhöyük Village, bounded to Polatlı County of Ankara. Its original name is Gorda. Perhaps, it is supposed that it becomes Gordion by adding "ion" suffix, which means "place" in Helen language. Gordion is the capital city of Phrygians. Phrygians (B.C. 750- B.C. 300) is a folk with Balkan origin. Firstly they come into existence in B.C. 750. They establish a state in a region between

Gordion

Eskişehir and Afyon. Their first emperor is Gordias. Their last emperor is famous Midas, who becomes subject of many myths. Cimmerians terminate Phrygian State in B.C. 695. However, Phrygian Art continues until B.C. 300. Remains, unearthed as a result of excavations, made in Gordion, show all features of Phrygian architecture. Furthermore, there are many tumulus around Gordion. Some of them are excavated. Metal and wooden works, unearthed from the excavation of Great Tomb of King Midas, show how Phrygians are advanced in these art branches. Works of Archaic Bronze, Hittite, Phrygian, Persian, Lydian, Hellenistic and Roman periods, which are unearthed from Gordion excavations, are exhibited in Gordion Museum.

PHRYGIAN ROCK MONUMENTS

"Phrygian Rock Monuments", which are among the most important works belonging to Phrygians, are located in the region, which is called Phrygian Valley between Eskisehir and Afyonkarahisar provinces. There are a lot of works caved in rocks in the city of Midas, in the vicinity of Eskişehir. The most important opus here is an outdoor temple, which is actually constructed for goddess Cybele and called Midas Monument, or Written Rock. Besides Midas city, Sümbüllü Monument, Yılantaş Monument, Aslankaya Monument (Cybele Outdoor Temple), "Aslantaş" lion reliefs, Maltaş Monument, Kapıkaya Monument are some of the other monuments. Furthermore, there are a lot of rock tombs caved in rocks, churches, houses etc. belonging to various periods and fairy chimneys, constituted by the nature, in Phrygian Valley. Collections, containing extremely rich archaeological and ethnographic works, belonging to various periods, are exhibited in Eskisehir Museum and especially Afyonkarahisar Archeological Museum and Afyonkarahisar Turkish and Islamic Arts Museum.

Phrygian monuments

Kütahya

KÜTAHYA

First settlement starts in Kütahya and surrounding since prehistoric ages and it is seen that Kütahya and surrounding are ruled firstly by Hittites by beginning from B.C. 1500 and then respectively Phrygians, Lydians, Persians, Macedonians, Bithinians, Kingdom of Pergamon and bounded to Roman Empire in B.C. 1st Century. It remains boundaries of Eastern Roman Empire in A.D. 395 and it becomes bishopric center in Christianity period. Kütahya witnesses Arabian blockade in 7th Century, going between Anatolian Seljuks and Byzantine in 11th Century, Crusades in 12th Century, Mongol invasion in 13th Century and the city enters under rule of Germiyen Oğulları between 1300-1428 after Anatolian Seljuks Empire enters into the process of destruction. Kütahya is included into Ottoman lands just in 1428. Name of Kütahya in ancient age is Kotiaeion. This word changes its form and becomes Kütahya in the course of time. Kütahya Castle, with three sections as upper castle, lower castle and citadel, located on a hill in the vicinity of Kütahya, is constructed in Byzantine period and fortified and repaired in Germiyen Oğulları and Ottoman periods. Some of historical and architectural structures in the city are 1377 dated Kurşunlu Mosque, 1410 dated Ulu Mosque, 1390-1428 dated Yakup Bey Social Complex, composed of Madrasah, small mosque and soup kitchen; and Vecidiye Madrasah, which is constructed in the early periods of Germiyen Oğulları. Besides these, there are a lot of historical mosques, small mosques, complexes, madrasah, tombs, hostelry in the city. Moreover, Kütahya Museum, Tile Museum and Kossuth Residence Museum (Hungarian House) are among the places, which are required to be visited in the city.

AIZANOI / Çavdarhisar

Aizanoi ancient city is located in Çavdarhisar County, in 54 km. far from Kütahya Province. Koca Stream, which is called Rhyndakos in the ancient age, passes through the city. Ancient city is located in two sides of this Stream and two sides are connected to each other with bridges, which are also used in these days. One part of Cavdarhisar County is located on ancient Aizanoi city. As Çavdar clans settle here during the period of Ertuğrul Ghazi in 13th century, here is called Çavdarhisar. History of ancient city dates back B.C. 1st century. City lives its most prime period in A.D. 2nd Century. Aizanoi becomes bishopric center in Christianity period. The most important structure in the city is Temple of Zeus, which is constructed in Ion order during the period of emperor Hadrian (117-138) in A.D. 2nd Century and stood magnificently in these days. But, this temple was joint temple of Mother Goddess and Zeus. The half of the temple which fronts to the east, belongs to Main Goddess and the other half of the temple which fronts to the west, belongs to Zeus. Other structures, located in the ancient city, are Bridges, connecting two sides of city to each other, Agora and Heroon, constructed in Dor order, Gymnasium, Baths, Round Structure, Bath Building, Stadium and Theatre Complex and Colonnaded Street.

Aizanoi-Çavdarhisar

Mevlana Tomb-Konya

KONYA

Name of Konya means "City of Icons", which is 'Ikonion" in Greek language. The oldest settlement place in Konya is the tumulus, called Alaeddin Hill within the city. First settlements here date back B.C. 2000 years according to obtained findings. The oldest settlement place around Konya is Çatalhöyük, which dates back B.C. 6500 years. There are Hittite and Phrygia settlement places in Konya and surrounding. City, which enters under Persian rule in B.C. 546, is included into territories of respectively Alexander the Great in B.C. 334 and Roman Empire in B.C. 133. City is exposed to Arabian invasions in A.D. 7th Century. It becomes the capital city of Anatolian Seljuks Empire in 1098. It is exposed to Mongol invasion in 1243. Anatolian Seljuks Empire goes out of existence in 1308. Region is ruled by Karamanoğulları Beylic. Konya is included into Ottoman lands during the reign of Fatih Sultan Mehmet in 1467.Konya lives its most prime period in 12th and 13th centuries under the rule of Anatolian Seljuks Empire and city is furnished with many architectural structures. Alaeddin Mosque, whose construction is completed during reign of I. Alaeddin Keykubat in 1221, and a tomb in which eight Seljuks sultans are buried, and Alaeddin Kiosk in the form of remains, are located on Alaeddin Hill. No remains of walls, surrounding the city, reach today. We see some reliefs and sculptures of these walls only in the museums. 1258 dated Sahip Ata Mosque, 1274 dated Seyh Sadreddin Konevi Mosque, 1156 dated Iplikci Mosque, 1230 dated Hatuniye Mosque, 1242 dated Sircali Madrasah, 1251 dated Karatay Madrasah, 1258 dated Ince Minaret Madrasah; Selimiye Mosque, constructed in 1565 in Ottoman period are some of the other important architectural structures in the city. Valuable works are exhibited in Archaeological and Ethnographic Museums in the city. Moreover, Tile Arts Museum in Karatay Madrasah, Tomb Monuments Museum in Sırçalı Madrasah; Seljuks Period, Stone and Wooden Arts Museum in Ince Minaret Madrasah; Mevlana Museum and Home of Ataturk Cul-

Views from Mevlana Tomb

ture Museum are among the other museums in Konya. The most important opus, located in Konya, is Mevlana Tomb, which is the symbol of Konya due to historical identity of Mevlana Celaleddin Rumi'nin (1207-1273). Tomb is constructed in 1274 and its architect is Bed-reddin Tebrizi. Tomb, coated with fluted body and 16 sliced an edged cone, is located within a group of structures (complex), constructed in Seljuks and Ottoman period. Besides Mevlana Tomb, other sections such as Reading room, Semahane, Small Mosque, Dervish cells, Matbah, are located within the group of structures. Mevlana Dergah is turned into the museum in 1927 and opened for public visits under the name of "Mevlana Museum". Works related to Mevlana and Mevleviyeh; and Turkish-Islamic arts are exhibited in the museum.

Salt Lake

LAKE TUZ

Lake Tuz (salt) is in the Middle Anatolia region in the northeast of the lowest part of the land surrounded by Kizilirmak in the east, Obruk plateau in the south, Cihanbeyli plateau in the west and Haymana plateau in the north. It is the second biggest lake inTurkey after Lake Van. The lake, which is tectonic geologically, has a closed basin. Although it is the second biggest lake, it is very shallow. In most places it is not deeper than 0.5 meters. During the spring months when water is ample, it gets as big as 164,200 hectares. The area has the driest weather in Turkey, and because it does not often rain it is not rich in rivers. Water sources include the Baglica and Kirdelik streams from the south, Esmekaya spring, Insuyu stream from the west and Pecenek stream from east. However, almost all of these sources dry up before reaching the lake in the summer. Nearly the whole lake desiccates during the summer as a result of extreme evaporation. In dry parts, a layer of salt in 30-centimeter thick is formed. It is one of the saltiest lakes in the world, as well as in Turkey. The density of the water is 1.225 g/cm3, and the percentage of salt in the water is 32.4%. There is no vegetation in the lake as a result of the amount of the salt in the water. However, it is possible to see scant plants that are resistant to salt in the areas near the freshwater streams. Most of Turkey's salt is obtained from here. It is one of the riches areas of Turkey in terms of the number of birds. The wide space that the lake takes up during the winter constitutes a vital winter shelter for water birds. There are also other marsh lands that are ecologically related to Lake Tuz such as Kulu Golu, Samsam Golu, Uyuz Golu, Kozanli Saz Golu, Boluk Golu, Tersakan Golu, Esmakaya Golu and the reservoir of the Hirfanli dam. These lakes that are very close to each other, and that they all have their own characteristics, constitute a marsh land complex that support a wide variety of wildlife with different habitat needs by feeding them and giving them a place to reproduce. This makes Lake Tuz very important. Around the lake, aside from the flamingos, avocets and angits that have adapted themselves to the salty waters, plovers, cranes, wild geese and wild ducks exist in large groups around the lake. Since the lake and the vicinity is relatively uninhabited, they can feed themselves easily and swim in the water of the lake, which does not freeze, even on the coldest days of the winter. Small islands in the lake create a very good sanctuary for birds, such as swamp swallow, drake, angit, kilicgaga, camurcun, kocagoz and different types of seagulls, during the incubation period. Lake Tuz is the most important brooding area for flamingos in Turkey. There are colonies of birds in middle the lake with approximately 5,000-6,000 nests that are used during incubation period.

AKSARAY(Archelais)

Aksaray name of which comes from Archelaos, the last king of the Cappadocia, is 60 miles northeast of the city of Konya. It is 980m from the sea level and it is a beautiful city with its rich history. Some sources also suggest that the name comes from the white palace that one of the Seljuk sultans, İzettin Kılıçarslan, built in 1202. The monuments, castles and their legends tell us that the region that Aksaray is in was under the control of the Hittites for a very long time. The Hellene name of the city was Garsaura that comes from the Hittite word Kursaura that meant the holy river in Hittite language. It was an important city during both Seljuks and Romans as it was in a position to control the ways that connect Kayseri to Capadocia and Ankara to Taurus Mountains. The city was under Karamanoğlu rule for a while. Eventually, Ottomans took control of the city. The major historical buildings and places include Ulu Mosque that was built by Seljuks and renovated by Karamanoglu İbrahim Bey, Zinciriye Medresah that is a museum today, Nakkaşi Mosque, Eğri Minaret, Taptuk Emre Tomb, Ziyaret Hill, Yüksek Church, Paşa Turkish Baths, Ziga Hot Springs, and Roman and Byzantine structures that were built on the skirts of Hasan Mountain and the ancient city of Nora (Viranşehir). It is one of the valuable cities of Capadocia region with its history extending back to 8000 BC,

Sultanhanı

NEVŞEHİR(Nenassa)

The city was founded by Frigs. Persians and Macedonians turned it into a major city. After Romans and Byzantines, Seljuks took control of the city after the year 1071. Sejuks actually called the city "Muskara". It is in the Kizilirmak valley that goes through Nevsehir and on the plateaus that are in the north and south of this valley. The altitude of the city is between 500-1000m and most of the geological and historical wonders that we have mentioned in this book such as unique valleys, fairy chimneys, dwellings carved into the rock, underground cities, open air museums, and churches engraved into the rock are in the borders of this city. The region looks more like it actually belongs to a different planet other than Earth. The major historical monuments of the city include Nevşehir castle, Kuyu Mosque, Kaya Mosque and Kurşunlu Mosque.

Paşabağ

CAPPADOCIA

Cappadocia Region covers Nevşehir, Aksaray, Kırşehir, Kayseri, Niğde, Yozgat and Malatya provinces nowadays. When it is mentioned about historical and natural richness and beauties and also Cappadocia; Göreme, Ürgüp, Avanos, Uçhisar, Ortahisar, Çavuşin, Pasabağ, Zelve, Mustafapaşa (Sinassos), Derinkuyu and Kaymaklı, bounded to Nevşehir; Güzelyurt and Ihlara Valley, bounded to Aksaray; and Soğanlı Valley, located within boundaries of Kayseri province, are the first thought names and places. Furthermore, there are many underground settlements (city), mainly Derinkuyu and Kaymaklı. Findings, obtained from excavations, which are made on Musular and Aşıklı höyük in the vicinity of Kızılkaya village, bounded to Gülağaç County, Aksaray Province, show that first settlements in Cappadocia region date back B.C. 7000; settlements in Güvercin Kayası tumulus date back B.C. 8000. Script enters into Anatolia for the first time with establishment of a trade colony by Assyrians in Kültepe, located in the vicinity of Kayseri Province in Cappadocia region between B.C. 1950-1750. Region is ruled respectively by Hittites in B.C. 1650-1200 years, Phrygians in B.C. 750, Lydians in the middle of B.C. 7th Century, Persians in B.C. 546, Alexander the Great Empire in B.C. 333. Cappadocia People live as princedoms and feudalities after Alexander the Great Empire falls into pieces in B.C. 323, and they are ruled by Roman Empire in B.C. 17. Region, which enters under Anatolian Seljuks Empire rule, is captured certainly by Ottomans in 15th Century. Compositions, called Fairy Chimneys, occurred because volcanic tuff rock masses, which are created by lavas, emerging through eruption of Erciyes Mount and Hasan Mount and other mountains between these two mountains in the Middle Anatolia, are eroded by natural conditions such as rain and wind. These compositions, reflecting a different world, may be deemed as one of the most leading natural wonders of the world. Cappadocia, which means Land of Beautiful Horses, is important in terms of history and nature as well as it is very important region in terms of religion. Although Christianity begins in A.D. 1st Century, Cappadocia becomes the center of Christianity religion by beginning from A.D. 3rd Century. It is the region of Churches, Saints and Church Fathers. Besides Saint Georgios, other famous saints of Cappadocia are mainly as follows: Great Saint Basileios from Kayseri, Saint Gregorios from Nisa and Saint Gregorios from Nazianzos. Fairy Chimneys, rock churches, underground cities and Göreme are the first thought places when it is mentioned about Cappadocia. There are various structures, dated as 9th, 10th and 11th Century and beginning of 12th Century and caved in rocks in Göreme outdoor museum and outside the museum. We can list some of them as follows. Adsız Church, Elmalı Church, St. Barbara Church, Yılanlı Church, Chapel, Karanlık Church, St. Catherina Church, Çarıklı Church, Maidens Monastery and dining Hall locations are located in Göreme outdoor museum. Tokalı Church, The Virgin Mary Church, Saklı Church, El Nazar Church and Kılıçlar Church, located in Göreme Valley outside Outdoor Museum, are among the other important churches. Among these churches, Karanlık Church, belonging to middle of 11th Century, is in Greek cross plan with two floors and four columns and central dome and with three abscissas and Birth of Jesus, Deisis, Crucifying and Ascension scenes are attractive among various scenes, belonging to Jesus's life, on the frescos inside it. Furthermore, some scenes, received from Old testament, are also depictured. Life of Jesus is explained with depictures on the frescos of Tokali Church, which is the biggest church of the region and constructed in 10th Century. Çarıklı Church, belonging to 11th Century, is constructed with two floors. There are three rooms in the ground floor and main church is on the upper floor. Scenes, which are received from life of Jesus and some subjects of Old testament are depictured in the frescos on the walls of this church. Elmalı Church, dated as middle of 12th Century, is constructed with four columns and with single nave in the plan of Greek cross. Scenes belonging to life of Jesus, and some scenes, which are received from Old testament, are also depictured in the frescos of this church. St. Barbara Church, dated as first half of 11th Century, is constructed according to covered Greek cross plan. Depictures of Pantokrator Jesus, St.

Uçhisar

Dark Church

Georgios and Theodoros and St. Barbara are located on the frescos. Yılanlı Church, dated as 11th Century, has two sections, there is a gate with two columns and vault, dividing two sections from each other. Deisis scene is located in the abscissa section and depictures of St. Onosimos, St. Georgios and St. Theodoros, and also emperor Constantinus and his mother Helena are situated in the left in the entrance. El Nazar Church, dated as 10th Century, is devastated substantially due to stroke of lightning and undergoes repair. It has two floor and depictures of Jesus, angles and saints are located inside it. Jesus is depicted inside a medallion, surrounded with angles, in the dome of church. Uçhisar and Ortahisar towns are located between Nevşehir and Göreme. These towns are named after castles near them. Ortahisar town attracts attention with historical castle, monasteries and churches. Uçhisar castle attracts attention with its houses caved in rocks. It is the attraction center for domestic and foreign visitors due to fairy chimneys, underground settlements, houses caved in rocks around Ürgüp. There are works, belonging to Seljuks and Ottoman period, and also a museum, in which archaeological and ethnographic works are exhibited, in the county. Stone houses, Holy Apostles Church, Keşlik Church,

Views from Tokalı Church

Ortahisar

St. Basil Church, Tavşanlı Church, belonging to 19th Century, are the places, which are required to be visited in Mustafapaşa, whose old name is Sinossos. Furthermore, Çavuşin, Zelve Outdoor Museum and Paşabag are the important places, which are required to be visited. There are about 50 churches and monasteries, which are constructed in different sizes between 9th and 13th centuries in Soğanlı Valley. Some of these churches are Karabaş Church, Tokalı Church, Yılanlı Church, St. Georgios Church, Azize Barbara Church, Kubbeli Church. There are about 36 churches in Ihlara Valley, in the length of 14 km. Sümbüllü Church, Ağaçaltı Church, Yılanlı Church, Kokar Church, are some of the important churches in this valley. Güzelyurt is also a small example of Cappodacioa with underground cities, churches, structures caved in rocks, Monastery Valley and fairy chimneys.Xenophon, who is one of the famous authors in ancient age, (B.C. 430-355), mentions about underground settlements in Cappadocia in his work, named as Anabasis. People, living in the region, were sheltering and hid here temporarily in order to protect their life and property in case of emergency or

El Nazar Church (Below)

Kılıçlar Valley

Derbent

A General View from Göreme (Below)

Monastery of the Virgins

war. Underground city were made by caving rocks and equipped in full. Everything for human requirement such as wide sheep fold for the animals, ventilation pipes, sitting places, worshipping places, bedrooms, kitchens, provisions stores, tandoori, fermented grape juice stores, toilets, communication channels with outside etc. are thought and constructed in the underground cities. There are about 200 underground settlements in the region. The biggest underground city in the region is Derinkuyu underground city in 29 km far away Nevsehir. Depth reaches to 85 m. in the underground city, whose 8 floors are opened for public visits. The other big underground city is Kaymaklı underground city, only four floors of this underground city, are brought into open. Özkonak, Saratlı, Acıgöl - Tatlarin, Mazı, Ağzıkarahan-Pınarbaşı, Özkonak - Saruhan hostel, Dolayhan Hostel and Til are some of the other underground cities.

Big hostels are constructed on the trade roads, passing through Cappadocia region in Anatolian Seljuks Empire period. Construction of Ağzıkara Hostelry, located between Aksaray-Nevşehir, is started between 1231-1236 dated during the period of I. Alaeddin Keykubad and it is completed during the period of Gıyaseddin Keyhüsrev in 1239. Sultan Hostelry, located between Aksaray and Konya, is constructed during the period of Seljuks Sultan I. Alaeddin Keykubat in 1229. Sultan Hostelry is the biggest one of Anatolian Seljuks hostelries and appears as a castle. Kiosk-small mosque, rooms, stores, bakery, hamam and barns are located inside it. Saruhan, located on Avanos-Ürgüp highway in 6 km. far away Avanos, is constructed during the period of Sultan II. İzzettin Keykavus in 1240. Avanos county, established along Kızılırmak, is known with its pots, hand woven carpets. In the provincial center of Nevşehir, Nevşehir Castle, Kaya Mosque

New Constructions -Uçhisar

Zelve

Soğanlı

Ihlara Canyon

Views from the Underground City Kaymaklı

Derinkuyu Underground City

and Nevşehirli Damat İbrahim Pasha Social Complex, constructed between 1718-1726, and Nevşehir Museum, in which archaeological and ethnographic works are exhibited; and also Hacı Bektaş Social Complex, which is constructed in 13th Century and brought into current position by extending with outbuildings in 16th Century in Hacıbektaş county in 47 km. north of Nevşehir and Museum inside it and also Hacıbektaş Archeological and Ethnography Museum are the other places, which are required to be visited.

Saratlı Underground City

A General View from Kayseri

KAYSERİ

Kayseri is established on a lowland in the northern foothills of Erciyes Mount in Middle Anatolia and it is in the position of an industrial city and first settlements around Kayseri date back B.C. 2500 years. This is proved by the findings, obtained from excavations, which are made in Kültepe in northern-east of the city. Furthermore, Kültepe is developed as Assyrian Trade Colony center between B.C. 1950 – B.C. 1750 and script is started to be used in Anatolia in this period for the first time and thus, Anatolia enters into history ages. Hittite and Phrygian settlements are also seen in the region. The first establishment place of Kayseri city is the top a hill in 2 km. southern-west of the city. Here is called "Mazaka". City, which enters under rule of respectively Persians in B.C. 546; Alexander the Great Empire in B.C. 333, falls to the share of Seleuceians when this empire is broken into pieces in A.D. 323. While Roman emperor Tiberius (14-37) makes Cappadocia as a Roman state, he calls the city as Caesarea / Kaisareia (Country of Caesarea). City is exposed to Arabian invasions in 7th Century, city is ruled by Seljuks soon after Battle Of Malazgirt in 1071. It is exposed to Mongol invasion in 13th Century and then city changes hands from time to time in the beylics period and it is included into Ottoman lands certainly during the reign of Yavuz Sultan Selim. Old structures, located in the city, belong to Seljuks and Ottoman period. Structures belonging to Roman and Byzantine period, can not reach today and they are destroyed. We can list important historical architectural structures in the city as follows. Although Kayseri Castle belongs to Byzantine period, it undergoes repair substantially in Seljuks and Ottoman period. Ulu Mosque, constructed during the period of Seljuks Sultan I. Gıyaseddin Keyhüsrev in 1206, Kölük Mosque, constructed in 12th Century, Hond Hatun Social Complex, composed of mosque, madrasah, tomb and bath during the period of Sultan II. Gıyaseddin Keyhüsrev in 1238, Döner large tomb, constructed for the name of daughter of sultan, Shah Cihan Hatun between 1276-1279, Çifte large tomb, constructed in 1247 by Ayyubids for the name of his daughter Melik-ül Ebubekir; and Melike Adiliye, who is wife of II. Keykavus, Kurşunlu Mosque, which is said to be constructed by Sinan the Architect, 1431-1432 dated Hatuniye Madrasah, Çifte Madrasah, composed of Nursing Home, constructed by the order of Gevher Nesibe in 1205, and school of medicine, constructed by the order of I. Gıyaseddin Keyhüsrev, Sahibiye Madrasah, constructed by the order of Seljuk vizier Fahreddin Ali Sahib Ata in 1267, Saraceddin Madrasah, constructed by the order of Emir Saraceddin Bedri in 1238 and Sırçalı Large Tomb, Covered Bazaar, Vezirhan, Pamukhan, Paşa Bath and Kadı Bath are some of the old architectural structures in Kayseri. Furthermore, Karatayhan, which is located between Kayseri and Malatya, outside Kayseri province on the trade roads, is constructed by Seljuk vizier Celaleddin Karatay in 1240-1241 years and Great Sultan Hostelry, located between Kayseri and Sivas, is constructed during the period of I. Alaeddin Keykubad between 1232-1236. Alayhan, lcoated between Kayseri and Aksaray, is also one of the other important structures in Kayseri. Moreover, Archaeological Museum and Ethnography Museum and Atatürk Museum, in which various cultures are exhibited from chalcolithic period to Byzantine period, are the other places, which are required to be visited, in Kayseri.

SİVAS

It is understood from archeological excavations, made around Sivas that first settlement started in the region since prehistoric ages. The name of the city in ancient age is Sebasteia. This name is given to the city by Pythodoris, who is the daughter of Pontus king VI Mitradathes, reigning between B.C. 120-63. City enters under Roman Empire rule in B.C. 63. Name of Sivas is also originated from Sebasteia. City, developing in Roman period, becomes state center in Byzantine period. City is exposed to Sassanian and Arabian robberies in 7th Century. City enters under rule of Danişmend Oğulları and Anatolian Seljuks in 11th Century. City, which is exposed to Mongol invasion in 1243, is ruled by İlhanlılar, Ottomans and after Timur invasions, it enters under Ottoman rule again in 1408. Neither wall nor trace of Sivas Castle, which is located in the southern-west of Sivas and repaired and used in Roman, Byzantine, Danişmendliler and Anatolian Seljuks periods, reaches today. Sivas is the one of the cities, which have the most beautiful architectural structures of Anatolian Seljuks period. Some of the most important ones are as follows: 1197 dated Ulu Mosque, belonging to period of Danişmendliler, 1271 dated Gök Madrasah, belonging to Anatolian Seljuks period, Buriciye Madrasah and Double Minaret Madrasah (Darülhadis), and also 1217 dated Izzeddin Keykavus Madrasah and Hospital and Keykavus Tomb in the Hospital, 1347 dated Güdük Minaret (Şeyh Hasan Bey Tomb), belonging to the period of Eretna Oğulları, 1319 dated Ahi Emir Ahmet Large Tomb are some of other works of Seljuks period in the city.Some of the other works belonging to Ottoman period in the city are as follows: 1562 dated Meydan Mosque (Çukur Mosque), belonging to Ottoman period, 1580 dated Castle Mosque and Ali Ağa Mosque, Abdülvahap Gazi Tomb, belonging to II. Bayezit period, 1600 dated Kara Şemseddin Aziz Tomb, Mehmed Efendi Hamam, belonging to beginning of 16th Century, Meydan Bath, belonging to 16th century, 1576 dated Kurşunlu Hamam, 1573 dated Behram Pasha Hostelry and Subaşı Hostelry. Congress Building, Atatürk and Ethnography Museum, Archaeological and Stone Arts Museum, Akaylar Residence Museum and İnönü Ethnography Museum are the museums, located in the city.

DİVRİĞİ

Divriği is situated in 168 km. far away Sivas through highway and it is known first settlement started in Divriği and surrounding since B.C. 1500. Name of city is called Tephrike for the first time in Byzantine period. It is known that this name changes and transforms into Divriği in the course of time. Furthermore, it passes as Divrik in some sources. Divriği, which is exposed to invasions of firstly Sasanians and then Arabians in 7th Century, enters under Turks rule after Battle of Malazgirt in 1071. Kemah, Erzincan, Şebinkarahisar and Divriği are given Mengücük Ghazi. When Mengücük Oğulları is divided into two branches in 1142, branch of Divriği is ruled by Mengücük Bey Süleyman. Divriği is ruled by Anatolian Seljuks firstly and then respectively İlhanlılar, Mem-

Double-Minaret Madrasah -Sivas

luks, Ottomans, Timur, again Memluks and finally it is included into Ottoman lands certainly in 1516. The most beautiful works, which are constructed by Mengücük Oğulları in Divriği, date between 1180-1277 years. The most beautiful opus, remaining from Mengücük Oğulları in Divriği, is Ulu Mosque and Hospital group of structures. This group of structures is composed of the mosque, which is constructed in 1228 by the order of Ahmed Shah, son of Mengücük Bey Süleyman Shah during the period of I.Alaeddin Keykubat and Hospital, which is constructed by the order of his wife Melike Turan in the same year and tomb, belonging to them. The architect of the structure is Hürrem Shah from Ahlat. Mosque is composed of five naves, which are vertical to niche wall. It is covered with twenty five vaults and domes. 1241 dated epigraph and name of Ahmet from Tbilisi are situated on the pulpit. A portal is located in each of east, west and north walls of the mosque. These portals are decorated with herbal motifs with rich reliefs. It is understood from the epigraph at the gate of Hospital near the Mosque that Hospital is constructed for Hürrem Shah by the order of Melike Turan. Hospital has a gothic style Portal in the western direction. Ahmed Shah and his wife Melike Turan are buried in the tomb with domes at the north-east corner of the Hospital. 1181 dated Castle Mosque, belonging to Mengücük Oğulları, Aşağı Bath, repaired in 1667, Bekir Çavuş Bath, belonging to 13th Century, 1241 dated Kemankeş Tomb, 1196 dated Kamerüddin Tomb are some of other works in Divriği county. Castle, which is located on the rocky place at the north of Divriği, is constructed in 1236-1237 by Ahmet Shah, son of Süleyman Shah from Mengücük Oğulları. Castle is composed of citadel and bailey. Walls of the castle have been demolished substantially.

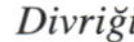

Divriği

A General View from Çorum

ÇORUM

First settlements around Çorum date back beginning of B.C. 3rd thousand year. Remains belonging to Early Bronze Age (B.C. 3000- B.C. 2500) are detected at the end of excavations, made in Alacahöyük and Boğazköy. While region is ruled firstly by Hittites in B.C. 2nd thousand and then respectively Phrygians, Persians, Alexander the Great; Romans in B.C. 1st century; Eastern Roman, after A.D. 395, Danişmend Oğulları in 1075, it is bounded to Anatolian Seljuks Empire during the period of II.Kılıçaslan in 1178. City, which is exposed to Mongol invasion in 13th Century, is included into Ottoman lands by Yıldırım Bayezit in 1389. Çorum Castle, located in the city, Ulu Mosque, constructed by the order of Hayreddin Nazır, who is emancipated slave of Alaeddin Keykubat, 1561 dated Hamid Mosque, 1579 dated Gülabibey Mosque, 1436 dated Old Bath, 1573 dated Ali Pasha Bath, 1494 dated Taceddin Pasha Bath and 1895 dated Clock Tower are some of the old works in the city. Çorum Museum, in which archaeological and ethnographic works are exhibited, is also one of the important places, which are required to be visited.

HATTUSA / Boğazkale

Hattusa is the capital city of Hittites, establishing the first state in Anatolia between B.C. 1650- B.C. 1200 years, and using the script for the first time as the state, and remains of Hattusa are in Boğazkale, bounded to Çorum province. Hattusa excavations are started in 1906. Excavations are still carried out by German scientists. City is located on a rough terrain and its lower city section is in the north and its upper city (acropolis) section is in the south. We can list important remains, which are required to be visited in the city, as follows: In lower city; settlement place, remaining from Karum Hattus period, dated as B.C. 19th-18th Century and Temple of Celestial God and Arinna Sun Goddess, Buyukkale, located in Acropolis, belongs to B.C. 14th and 13th centuries and walls, city and acropolis gate, tunnel, courtyards, place buildings, halls, Hittite Emperial archive building, temples and the other remains are situated here. Remains of Hittite Castle, dated as B.C. 13th Century in Nişan Hill out of Büyükkale, King Gate and Gate with Lions, dated as beginning of B.C. 14th Century on the walls, surrounding the city, and also Yer Gate, Gate with Sphinx; Yenice Castle, dated as B.C. 13th Century, Sarı Castle and Boğazköy Museum in the region are the places which are required to be visited. One of the most important places,

Yazılıkaya

Boğazkale

which are required to be visited, is Yazılıkaya, which is a natural and outdoor temple in 2 km. northern-east of Hattusa. Yazılıkaya, belonging to B.C. 13th Century, is a Hittite pantheon and all Hittite gods are depicted here.

ALACAHÖYÜK

Alacahöyük is located within boundaries of Alaca county, bounded to Çorum. It is detected in the excavations, made here in 1935, that there is a settlement, which dates back B.C. 4th thousand. Valuable works, composed of golden, silver, bronze and cult symboles, unearthed from excavations, are exhibited in The Museum of Anatolian Civilizations in Ankara. Plaster copies of sphinxes, protecting City Gate and dated as Hittite Empire period (B.C. 1460- 1200), originals of orthostatics, decorating the city wall, are carried into The Museum of Anatolian Civilizations in Ankara. In spite of this, copies of orthostatics are made and put into their original places in Alacahöyük. Moreover, Alacahöyük Museum is one of the places, which are required to be visited here.

AMASYA / AMASEIA

First settlements in Amasya and surrounding date back B.C. 2000 years. Historical name of Amasya is Amaseia. We see this name for the first time at the end of B.C. 4th Century in the written sources in the history. After Macedonian Empire is divided in B.C. 323, Amaseia comes into prominence substantially during the period of Kingdom of Pontus (B.C. 302- 62), established in B.C. 302. I. Mithridates, establishing Kingdom of Pontus, makes Amaseia as capital city. City enters under Roman Empire rule in B.C. 63. City, which enters under Eastern Roman management in 395, is exposed to Arabian invasion in 7th Century and then even if it is captured by Byzantines again, it is ruled by Danişmendliler at the end of 11th Century and Anatolian Seljuks during the period of II. Kılıçaslan (1156-1192). It is exposed to Mongol invasion in 13th Century. Later on, it lives Beylics period. It is included into Ottoman lands by Yıldırım Bayezit in 1389. We can list the historical works in the city as follows. Amasya Castle on Harşema Mount is constructed during the period of Pontus King I. Mithridates (M.Ö.302-266).

Alacahöyük

Amasya

Although it is destroyed in Roman period (B.C. 69), it is also repaired in the subsequent periods and used in Seljuks and Ottoman periods. King Rock Tombs belong to B.C. 2nd Century and used as chapel in Byzantine period. Rock tunnel with stairs, constructed in B.C. 3rd -1st centuries, and Ferhat Aqueduct are the important historical works. Wreathed Minaret Mosque, constructed during the period of Gıyasettin Keyhüsrev II (1237-1247), Gökmedrese Mosque, composed of mosque, madrasah and tomb and constructed by Amasya Governor Seyfeddin Torumtay in 1266/67, Halifet Gazi Large tomb, constructed by the order of Halifet Alp İbni Tuli, one of the Seljuks emirs, 1242; Hospital, constructed by the order of Amber Abdullah in 1308/09; Çilehane, constructed by the order of Yakup Pasha in 1413 in Ottoman period, 1414 dated Bayezid Pasha Mosque; Yürgüç Pasha Mosque, constructed by the order of Yürgüç Pasha in 1428, 1486 dated Mehmed Pasha Mosque; and also Bayezit II social complex, composed of mosque, madrasah, soup kitchen, tomb, water-tank with a fountain and fountain and constructed in 1485/86, Kapı Ağa Madrasah, constructed by the order of Hüseyin Ağa, Gate Chief of II. Bayezit in 1488, Taşhan, constructed in 1698-1699, are some of the other old works in the city. Amasya Museum, in which archaeological and ethnographic works are exhibited, and Hazeranlar Residence, belonging to 19th Century and restored and opened for public visits as Museum-home in 1984, are the places, which are required to be visited.Strabon, who is the famous geographer of ancient age and living between B.C. 64 / 63 – A.D. 20 / 21, is from Amasya and 12th, 13th and 14th volumes of the work, which he writes as 17 volumes, are related to historical geography of Turkey.

Tokat

TOKAT

Researches in Tokat province and surrounding show that first settlements here date back prehistoric ages. Findings, belonging to calcolithic period, are unearthened in the excavations, made on Maşhat tumulus, bounded to Zile county in Tokat province. Although origin of Tokat name is not known certainly, it is said that it is derived from Dokeia. While Arabian geographer Ebu Abdullah Muhammed el-İdrisi, living in 12th Century, mentions about Anatolia, he also mentions about name of "Tokhat" province. City and surrounding is ruled firstly by Hittites by beginning from B.C. 1500, and then it is exposed to Assryian, Hurrian and Cimmerian invasions in the various periods. It enters under the rule of firstly Persians and then Macedonians, by beginning from B.C. 6th Century. Region, witnessing wars between Kingdoms of Cappadocia and Pontus, is included into Roman lands in B.C. 1st Century. Later on, Byzantine, Arabian invasions, Danişment Beylic, Mongol invasion, İlhanlılar period are lived. Tokat is included into Ottoman lands during the reign of Yıldırım Bayezit. City, which is lost by Ottoman Empire with Timur invasion in 1402, is included into Ottoman lands certainly during the reign of Fatih Sultan Mehmet.The most beautiful works in Tokat belong to Danişmendliler, Seljuks and Ottoman periods. Garipler Mosque, which is constructed in 1104 by Danişmend Ghazi, Çukur Madrasah, constructed by the order of Melik Nizameddin Yağıbasan in 1164, 1234 dated Ebül Kasım Tomb, 1250 dated Stone Bridge, constructed by the architect Bahaeddin Muhammed on Yeşilırmak, 1251 dated Seferbeşe Small Mosque and Tomb, 1292 dated Sümbülbaba Small Dervish Lodge and Tomb and Halef Sultan Small Dervish Lodge, Pervane Bath are some of the works of Seljuks period in the city. Pervan Bey Hospital, which is known as Gökmedrese today, is constructed in 1275. Hospital, which is constructed with two floors, also carries out its function in Seljuks and Ottoman periods. Gökmedrese serves as Tokat Museum, in which archaeological and ethnographic works are exhibited, in these days. 1412 dated Hamza Bey Mosque, constructed in Ottoman period; Meydan Mosque, constructed in 1485 by the order of Sultan II. Bayezit for the name of his mother Gülbahar Hatun; 1535 dated Bezhat Mosque; Ali Paşa Mosque, Bazaar, Çifte Han and Taşhan, constructed between 1565-1572, are some of the other works, belonging to Ottoman period. Tokat Castle is located on a steep hill in 6 km. north of Tokat. Castle, constructed in Byzantine period, are repaired and used by Danişmendliler, Seljuks and Ottomans. However, it is in the position of ruins in these days.

Amasra

AMASRA / AMASTRIS

According to the myth, city is established by Megarian immigrants in B.C. 6th Century with the name of Sesamos; as Persian princess Amastris, who is married to tyrant Dionysos from Herakleia Pontika (Karadeniz Ereğlisi), establishes the city again in Hellenistic period, the city is called with this name. Name of Amasra, which is a coastal town, bounded to Bartın province in Western Blacksea Region, is the changed form of Amastris name in the ancient age, in the course of time. After the management of Princess Amastris, city enters under the rule of firstly Kingdom of Pontus and then Roman Empire. Amasra becomes center of Bithynia-Pontus State in this period. Amasra witnesses great public works in A.D. 2nd Century. City, remaining within Eastern Roman boundaries in 395, is rented to Genoeses by Byzantines in 1270. City is included into Ottoman lands in 1460. City, located on an island and peninsula, is surrounded with walls and it is in the position of two castles. Castle on the island is known as Sormagir Castle and castle on the peninsula on the peninsula, is known as Zindan Castle. Both castles are connected to each other by Kemere Bridge, constructed in Roman period. Church, belonging to 9th Century on the castle, is turned into the mosque and called Fatih Mosque. Furthermore, a church, which is turned into a small mosque, is called Church Small Mosque. Amasra Castle is constructed again on the foundations of castle, belonging to Roman period in 9th Century and undergoes repair in Genoese and Ottoman periods. Therefore, there are some amblem reliefs, belonging to Genoese period, on the walls. Moreover, some structure remains belonging to various periods are seen in the city and its surrounding. İskele Mosque, Eyiceler Small Mosque and Ethem Ağa Residence are some of architectural structures, belonging to Ottoman period. Amasra Museum, in which works of Roman, Byzantine, Ottoman periods and local ethnographic works are exhibited, is located in the city.

SAFRANBOLU

Researches, which are made in some caves in Safranbolu and its surrounding, show that first settlements here date back paleolithic period. Region is ruled firstly by Hittites by beginning from B.C. 1500 years, and then Phrygians in B.C. 8th Century, and then respectively Cimmerians, Lydians, Persians, Macedonians, Bithynians, Romans and Byzantines, Anatolian Seljuks, Çobanoğulları Beylic, Candaroğulları. After

Safranbolu Houses

it witnesses Mongol invasion in 1243, it enters under rule of İlhanlılar and again Candaroğulları and finally Safranbolu is included into Ottoman lands in 1461. It is said that this name is given to Safranbolu because saffron herb is growing here. However, it is understood that name of city is Dadybra before Anatolian Seljuks Empire, Seljuks change it as Zalifre, and then it is used as Taraklı Borlu, Zağferanbolu, Zafranboli and finally it take the shape of Safranbolu, which is used today. All architectural structures, located in Safranbolu, belong to Candaroğulları and Ottoman periods. Substantial parts of these old architectural structures are repaired and put into service. 1322 dated Gazi Süleyman Pasha Mosque, belonging to Candaroğulları period, and said that it is turned from the church to mosque; and its madrasah and bath, Taşminare Mosque are some of the works, constructed in this period. Köprülü Mosque, constructed by the order of Köprülü Mehmet Pasha in 1661 in the Ottoman period, 1718 dated Hidayetullah Mosque, constructed by the order of Hidayet Aga, Dağdelen Mosque, 1779 dated Kazdağlı Mosque, 1796 dated İzzet Mehmet Pasha Mosque; Lütfiye Mosque, constructed by the order of Hacı Hüsnü Bey in 1878; 1884 dated Mescid Mosque, Kavaflar Bazaar (Arasta), Safranbolu Bazaar, Yemeniciler Bazaar, 1797 dated Clock Tower; District Governors House, serving as museum, 1648 dated Cincihan, 1845 dated Hacı Emin Efendi Tomb, 1871 dated Sheikh Mustafa Tomb, Köprülü

A General View from Safranbolu

Fountain, Salih Pasha Fountain, Sadullah Fountain, Pasha Pınarı Fountain are some of the old structures in the city. The most beautiful works of the city are "Safranbolu Houses", which are symbol and historical identity of the city. These houses, belonging to 18th and 19th century and made of stone and wooden, are protected and repaired and people are living in these houses today.

A General View from Kastamonu

KASTAMONU

Researches, which are made in the caves around Kastamonu, show that first settlements in this region date back Paleolithic age. Region is ruled respectively by Gasgas in the first half of B.C. 2nd thousand; Hittites in B.C. 1500; and then Phrygians in the middle of B.C. 8th Century. Later on, it is ruled respectively by Cimmerians, Persians, Macedonians, Pontus, Roman, Byzantines and then Kastamonu is ruled by Danişmendoğulları in 1105. Although city is captured by Byzantines for some time, city enters under Candaroğulları rule in 1213 and it is included into Ottoman lands during the reign of Yıldırım Bayezit. After Ottomans are beaten by Timur in 1402, Kastamonu, which is lost by Ottoman, is included into Ottoman lands certainly during the reign of Fatih Sultan Mehmet in 1461. Names such as Tumanna, Castumanna, Castrokommen, Kastomoni, Germanicopolis, Castonom are used for Kastamonu throughout history. Name of city passes as Kastamon in the works of Byzantine historians. It is supposed that name of city is derived from Kas-Ta-(u)ma wana (= Temple-belief-peoples'-Country).There are many old architectural structures, belonging to Çobanlar Dynasty (Kastamonu Atabeyleri), Candaroğulları and Ottoman periods in Kastamonu. We can list some of them as follows. Kastamonu Castle is constructed during the period of Byzantine period Komnenos Dynasty (1081-1185) and undergoes repair in Candaroğulları and Ottoman periods. 1273 dated Atabey Mosque and Atabey Tomb, 1272 dated Yılanlı Hospital, 1262 dated Frenkşah Bath, which is constructed as double bath by the order of Frenkşah Cemalüddin, are th works, belonging to Çobanlar Dynasty, among old architectural structures in Kastamonu. İbni Neccar Mosque, constructed by the order of Hacı Murat in 1353; İsmail Bey Social Complex, composed of mosque, madrasah, soup kitchen, hostelry, bath and tomb and constructed between 1454-1475; 1443 dated İbrahim Bey Mosque;

Castle Mosque, constructed by the order of İsfendiyar Bey between 1434-1435; Hamza Ağa Mosque, Hatun Sultan Tomb, Kurşunlu Hostelry (İsmail Bey Hostelry) are some of the works, belonging to Candaroğulları period. Nasrullah Mosque, constructed by the order of Nasrullah Kadı in 1506; Yakup Ağa Mosque and Madrasah, constructed by the order of Kilercibaşı Yakup Ağa in 1547; 1559 dated Ferhat Pasha Mosque, 1571 dated Sinan Bey Mosque; Münire (Bayraklı) Madrasah, constructed by the order of Hacı Mustafa Efendi in 1746; Clock Tower, Balkapanı Hostelry, Alem Hostelry, Urgan Hostlery, Yanık Hostelry Karanlık Bazaar, Çifte Hamam, Arabapazarı Çiftehamamı are the old architectural structures of Ottoman period in the city.Structure, which is used as Kastamonu Museum, is constructed in 1910 and it is the opus of famous architect of the period, the Architect Kemalettin Bey. Works, belonging to Kastamonu and surrounding provinces, in prehistoric ages, and Hittite, Phrygian, Hellenistic, Roman, Byzantine, Seljuks, Ottoman periods, and ethnographic material of the region and also documents related to the hat reform, are exhibited in the museum. Liva Pasha Residence, constructed by the order of Sadık Pasha between 1879-1881, serves as Ethnography Museum in these days. Furthermore, most of ancient houses and residences, located in Kastamonu, are under protection and some of them are repaired and opened for use. Sepetçioğlu Residence, Kırk Odalı Residence, Konyalı Residence, Mazlumcular Residence, İsmail Bey Residence, Toprakçılar Residence are some of these residences.

Kastamonu

Sinop

SİNOP

Researches, which are made around Sinop, show that first settlements here date back B.C. 4500 years. Name of Sinop passes as Sinuwa in Hittite documents. City, which is called Sinope in Hellen language, takes the shape of Sinop, which is used in these days. Sinop city is a colony city, established under the name of Sinope by Miletians in B.C. 756. After city is ruled by Phrygians, Cimmerians, Persians, Macedonians; city remains within boundaries of Pontus State in B.C. 303 and it becomes second capital city of Pontus State in B.C. 169. City, which enters under Roman rule in B.C. 67, remains under Easterm Roman (Byzantine) rule from 395 to 1213. Sinop is ruled respectively by Anatolian Seljuks Empire and Pervaneoğulları, between 1214 - 1292 and then Candaroğulları Beylic between 1292-1461. Sinop is included into Ottoman lands in 1461.

Sinop is a considerably rich city, in terms of old works. The most important opus is Sinop Castle. There are many works, belonging to Seljuks and Ottoman period. Sinop Castle is constructed during the period of Pontus King VI. Mithridates (B.C.120-63) in B.C. 72. The castle is composed of two sections which are citadel and bailey. While north walls of the castle protect the city from the sea, its land side is reinforced with a deep defense trench. The castle has four gates. There are epigraphs, belonging to Turk period, at north, east and south walls of the castle. While citadel serves as Sinop Jailhouse in Ottoman and Republic periods, it is also famous to host famous journalists and authors of the period. Alaeddin Mosque is constructed by the order of Alaeddin Keykubat in 1214. Palace Mosque, con-

Sinop(Above)

structed by the order of Candaroğlu Celalettin Bayezit in 1374, Cezayirli Ali Pasha Mosque, belonging to Seljuks period, Seyit Bilal Tomb, Meydan Kapı Mosque, 1353 dated Fetih Baba Small Mosque, 1648 dated Mehmet Ağa Small Mosque; Süleyman Pervane Madrasah, constructed by the order of Seljuks vizier Süleyman Pervane in 1262, 1322 dated Ghazi Çelebi Tomb, 1394 dated Sultan Hatun Tomb, İsfendiyaroğulları Tomb, 1289 dated Lion Fountain, 1358 dated Ulu Bey Fountain, 1448 dated İsmail Bey Fountain, are some of the other old works, located in the city. Works, belonging to ancient bronze, archaic, classic, Hellenistic, Roman, Byzantine periods, and also ethnographic works and icons of 19th century are exhibited in Sinop Museum.

Samsun(Below)

Samsun

SAMSUN

Researches, which are made around Samsun, show that first settlements here date back Paleolithic period. It is seen that region is ruled respectively by Hittites in B.C. 1500 years and then Phrygians in B.C. 8th Century. Samsun has also a very important position in the ancient ages because of having a single port and a large hinterland between Sinop and Trabzon in Black Sea Region. Samsun city is a colony city, established under the name of Amisos by Miletians at the beginning of B.C. 7th Century for the first time. Later on, while city is ruled respectively by Persians, Macedonians and then Pontus in B.C. 300, it is included into Roman lands in B.C. 47. After Roman Empire is divided into two pieces in 395, city remains within boundaries of Eastern Roman Empire and enters under Anatolian Seljuks Empire rule during the period of II. Kılıçaslan in 1185. However, original fortified section of the city remains under the control of Byzantine and Genoesians for about 200 years. After Mongol invasion in 1243, city is ruled by İlhanlılar. City is included into Ottoman lands during the period of Yıldırım Bayezit just at the end of 14th century. After Timur invasion in 1402, city, which enters under Candaroğulları Beylic rule, is included into Ottoman lands again certianly during the period of Çelebi Mehmet in 1427. Different names such as Aminsos, Amisos, Amisus, Enete, Sampson, Simisso,Sinusso, Peiraeus, Pire, Pompeiopolis are used for the city throughout the history. Old structures, located in the city, belong to İlhanlı, Candaroğulları and Ottoman periods. Yalı (Hoca Hayrettin) Mosque, constructed by the order of Sadık bin Abdullah in 1312, Castle Mosque, constructed in 1314 for the name of İlhanlı Governor Emir Timurtaş Pasha; Kurşunlu Mosque, constructed by the order of Molla Fahreddin in 1340; Hacı Hatun Mosque, constructed by the order of İbrahim, son of Hatice, in 1694; Büyük Mosque (Valide Mosque), constructed by the order of Batumlu Hacı Ali Efendi in 1884; Pazar Mosque, Hançerli Mosque, Sheikh Kudbeddin Mosque and Tomb, Çakıllı Hostelry, Taşhan are the other old works, located in the city. Works, belonging to region in chalcolithic, Ancient Bronze, Hittite, Hellenistic, Roman periods and ethnographic works, are exhibited in Archaeological and Ethnography Museum in Samsun. Furthermore, Atatürk Museum and Municipality Gazi Museum are situated in the city.

Ordu

ORDU

First settlement started in Ordu and its surrounding since ancient ages. Region is ruled firstly by Hittites in B.C. 1500 years and then Phrygians in 8th Century. Original and old settlement place of Ordu is Kotyora ancient city, called "Bozukkale", in 9 km northern-west of the city. Kotyora is a colony city, established in B.C. 7th Century. After it is ruled by Persians in B.C. 546 and then Macedonia in B.C. 333, it enters under Pontus rule in B.C. 300. Later on, while city is ruled respectively by Roman in B.C. 53, Eastern Roman in 395, Trabzon Greek (Roman) Empire in 1204, Hacıemiroğulları Beylic in 1270, it is included into Ottoman lands in 1427. City witnesses a conflagration in 1883. Old structures in the city, belong to after 19th century. 1800 dated İbrahim Pasha Mosque, 1891 dated Hamidiye Mosque and 1883 dated Yalı Mosque are some the old structures, located in the city. Furthermore, Orthodox Church, constructed in 1856 and located in the city, is opened for service as Cultural Center in 2000 after required repairs are performed. Paşaoğlu Residence, belonging to 19th Century, is also put into service under the name of Paşaoğlu Residence and Ethnography Museum in 1987 after required restoration activities are performed. "Green Ordu" title is used for the city because the city and its surrounding are covered with greneeries. There are a lot of lowlands such as Çambaşı, Perşembe, Argın, Keyfalan, Çukuralan, Taşkesik around the city. These lowlands offer unique beauties for incoming visitors.

Giresun

GİRESUN

First settlements in Giresun and its surrounding date back prehistoric ages. Region is ruled by Hittites in B.C. 1500 years and then Phrygians in B.C. 8th Century. A city is established under the name of Kerasos by Miletians colonies in 2 km. west of current Giresun city at the beginning of B.C. 7th Century. After Persian invasion in B.C. 6th Century and Macedonian rule in 333, Kingdom of Pontus, established in B.C. 302, starts to dominate the region. Pontus king Pharnakos I (B.C.185-169) surrounds and capture Giresun in B.C. 183. City, which is captured at the end of a challenging war, is destroyed substantially. Thereupon, king Pharnakos establishes a new city under the name of Pharnakeia on peninsula in 2 km. north of the city. City, which enters under Roman rule in B.C. 53, is called Kerasos again. Later on, it enters under the rule of respectively Eastern Roman in 395, Trabzon Greek (Roman) Empire in 1204, Kadı Burhaneddin Beylic in 1397, Ottomans in 1389. When Yıldırım Bayezit is beaten by Timur in 1402, Giresun is lost by Ottomans. Finally, Giresun is included into Ottoman lands certainly in 1461. Thus, Kerasos city is called Giresun. Different names such as Areitas, Area, Kerasos, Kerassonda, Kirezun, Kerasus, Pharnakeia, Pharnacia, Pharnas are used for Giresun throughout the history. Name of Kerasos is originated from Ceresia, growing in the environment. Giresun Castle is constructed in B.C. 4th-3rd centuries probably. Remains of palace, belonging to Pontus king I. Pharnakos, church and mosques and also Seyit Vakkas Tomb, belonging to 19th century, are located in the castle. Aretias Castle, which is subject of mythology, is located on the small island, located in the north of Giresun. Bogora Church, constructed in 18th century, is repaired and serves under the name of Giresun Museum. Works of Hellenistic, Roman, Byzantine, Ottoman periods and local ethnographic works are exhibited in the museum. 1830 dated Castle Mosque, 1861 dated Soğuksu Mosque, 1900 dated Şeyh Kerameddin Mosque, Hacı Mikdad Mosque, which is constructed in 1661 and renewed in 1889, are some of the old structures, located in the city. Ancient houses, located in Zeytinlik District of the city, are under protection. Kümbet Upland, Bektaş Upland, Kulakkaya Upland, Melikli Obası Upland, Karagöl Mountains and Uplands and many uplands within provincial boundaries of Giresun, offer unique beauties for the visitors. Uplands in Black Sea Region witness great festivals in the summer season.

Sumela Monastery-Trabzon

TRABZON

Trabzon has blue sea, green nature, historical richess and uplands and mountains like Alps, and it is established as a port city under the name of Trapezus, by Sinopes (From Sinop), who comes here in B.C. 756. However, as Sinop is also a Miletus colony city, it is said that Trabzon is established by Miletian colonies, not by Sinopes. Name of Trabzon passes in Anabasis (Retreat of Ten Thousands) named opus, written by Ksenophon (B.C. 430-355) for the first time. It is said that Trabzon word is originated from Trapezous word, which means "with plain" veya quadrangle shaped table in Greek language. City, which enters under Persian rule in B.C. 546, is ruled by Alexander the Great in B.C. 333 however, after this empire is broken into pieces in B.C. 323, it remains within boundaries of Pontus State, whose center is Amaseia in B.C. 280. After Romans destroy Pontus

State, city enters under Roman Empire rule. Great public works are seen in the city especially during the period of emperor Hadrian (117-138). After Roman Empire is divided into two pieces in 395, it remains within boundaries of Eastern Roman Empire. Kommenos dynasty Alexius, who escapes from Istanbul upon invasion of Latins during Crusades in 1204, comes to Trabzon and establishes Trabzon Greek (Roman) Empire here. After Trabzon is captured by Fatih Sultan Mehmet, it is included into Ottoman Empire lands in 1461. It is known that walls, beginning from seaside and surrounding Trabzon, exist in B.C. 5th Century. Walls are

Ayasofya Museum-Trabzon

extended in Byzantine period and repaired in Ottoman period. Trabzon Castle is composed of three sections such as Yukarıhisar (Citadel), Ortahisar and Aşağıhisar. The most important opus in Trabzon is Hagia Sophia Church, constructed between 1250-1260. This church is turned into the mosque in 1670, and it is used as military headquarters, hospital and store for some time during The First World War, structure is restored between 1958-1962 years and it is turned into museum in 1964. Church which is constructed at east-west direction with cross plan, is composed of narthex, cella and two lateral naves and three abscissas, of which those in sides are small and one in the middle is big. Hagia Sophia has three entrances with cloisters at north, south and west. Scenes, received from the Bible and Old Testament, are depictured on the frescos, decorating inside the church. Reliefs, showing creation of Adam and Eve, are located in the frontal on the southern entrance of the church. Quadrangle shaped Bell Tower, situated in the side of main structure, is constructed in 1427. Kostaki Residence, which is used as Trabzon Museum, is constructed by Italian architects, by the order of banker Aleksi Kostaki Teohyplaktos between 1898-1913 years. Residence is put into service as Trabzon Museum, in which archaeological and ethnographic works are exhibited, in 2001. Structure, which is located in Soğuksu district and known as Atatürk Kiosk, is constructed as summer kiosk by the order of Konstantin Kabayanidis between 1890-1903. Kiosk is turned into the museum in memory of Ataturk in 1964. There are many old structures inside the city. We can list some of them as follows: Aqueducts belonging to Byzantine period, Tabakhane Bridge, Zağnos Bridge, 1514 dated Gülbahar Hatun Mosque and Tomb, Arsenal, 1529 dated İskender

Uzungöl-Trabzon

Pasha Mosque, Küçük Ayvasıl Church, belonging to 7th Century; Maiden's Monastery, Ortahisar / Fatih Mosque (Panaghia Chrysocephalos Church), which is turned from church to the mosque; Yeni Cuma Mosque (St. Eugenios Church), Nakip Mosque (St. Andrea Church); Santa Maria Church, constructed between 1869-1874; Bazaar, Taşhan and also Trabzon Houses under protection, are some of the old works in the city. The most important opus outside provincial center of Trabzon is Sumela Monastery, located in Altıdere Valley within boundaries of Maçka county. A rock church is constructed in front of wide cavity like a cave of a steep rock for the name of The Virgin Mary by priest Barnabas and Sophronios in 385 and constitution of Sumela Monastery is provided. Monastery is extended during the period of Emperor Iustinianos (527-565), monastery gains great importance during the period of Trabzon Greek (Roman) Empire, established in 1204, and coronation of emperor III. Alexius (1349-1390) is organized here. After Trabzon enters under the control of Ottomans in 1461, Monastery continues its normal life until 1923. Monastery is abandoned due to the population Exchange with Greece after war. Sümela Monastery, which is neglected for long period, is taken under protection in 1972. Its required repairs and conservation works are performed and it is open for public visits in these days. Aqueducts are situated in the entrance of monastery and main church, guesthouse, library, student rooms, kitchen, spring, guardian rooms, bell tower and the other structures are located inside the monastery. Frescoes, decorating internal and external walls of main church, contain scenes, received from the Bible and Old Testament. Besides Sumela Monastery, there are important monasteries such as Kuştul, Kaymaklı and Vazelon in Trabzon region. Wonder of nature Uzungöl, which is located within boundaries of Çaykara County in 99 km far from Trabzon and composed as a result of landslide, is one of the most popular touristic places of Trabzon and has equal beauties like European Alps. Furthermore, Karadağ, Hıdırnebi, Sis Mount, Kadırga, Sultan Murat, Düzköy (Haçka nomad camping side), Maçka/Şolma Upland and the other uplands offer unique beauties to the visitors. Furthermore, these uplands witness great festivals in the summer season.

Rize

RİZE

Surface researches, made in Rize and its surrounding, show that first settlements here date back prehistoric ages. Cimmerians come to the region in B.C. 8th Century. Rize city is established by Miletians colonies, who come here in the middle of B.C. 8th Century for the first time. Rize and the region, in which it is located, enter under rule of firstly Medians in B.C. 6th Century and then Persians in B.C. 546. Later on, it enters under rule of respectively Macedonians in B.C. 333, Kingdom of Pontus in B.C. 280, Roman Empire in B.C. 63, Eastern Roman Empire in 395. City, which is exposed to Arabian invasions in 7th Century, remains under boundaries of Trabzon Greek (Roman) Empire, established in 1204. It is included into Ottoman lands by Fatih Sultan Mehmet in 1461. Name of city is used as Rizaion (in Latin writing, as Rhizaion) in Byzantine age. "Riza-ion" means "Place of Riza" in Greek language. Source of Rize name must be this word. After castle, which is located here in advance, is destroyed due to war and natural conditions, Rize Castle is constructed again on foundations of this old castle by Genoesians between 1314-1330. Castle is composed of two sections as Citadel and Lower Castle. Lower Castle is destroyed substantially. İslam Pasha Mosque, which is constructed during the reign of Yavuz Sultan Selim at the beginning of 16th Century, Gülbahar Hatun Mosque, constructed by the order of Gülbahar Hatun, mother of Yavuz Sultan Selim; 1570 dated Cafer Pasha Mosque, constructed by the order of Cafer Pasha, are some of the other old structures, located in the city. House of Mehmet Mataracı, in which Mustafa Kemal stays while he is coming to Rize in September 17, 1924, is restored and used as Atatürk House and Ethnography Museum. Some articles, belonging to Ataturk and local ethnographic works are exhibited in the museum. Furthermore, there are a lot of uplands within boundaries of Rize province. Anzar (Ballıköy), Çağırankaya, Palovit, Ayder, Apivanak Uplands are some of them. Kaçkar Mountains are among the important sightseeing places.

Girlevik Waterfall-Erzincan

ERZİNCAN

Erzincan is established on the flat and fertilized lowland, surrounded with high mountains. First settlement started in the region since B.C. 2000 years. It witnesses big earthquake-deaths and tragic events down the ages up to now because it is located on the fault line in terms of its geological structure. This case prevents development of city and increase of population. Erzincan and its surrounding is ruled respectively by Hittites, Urartians, Medians, Persians, Arabians, Eastern Romans (Byzantines), Seljuks, Akkoyunlular, Ottomans and finally Republic of Turkey State throughout the history. As it is destroyed and reconstructed due to the earthquakes, historical structures are not seen in the city. However, it is possible to see some structure remains in old Erzincan settlement area, which is abandoned due to the earthquake. Altıntepe site, which is an important settlement place belonging to Urartians, establishing a great state in Eastern Anatolian Region between B.C. 900-600 years, is located in 15 km. east of the city. Temple, palace, columned reception room, outdoor temple and graves are the important remains, unearthed as a result of excavations, which are made here by Prof. Dr. Tahsin Özgüç, who is the one of the lecturers of Ankara University Faculty of Language and History- Geography. Urartians advanced in metal art very much. Especially their vessels with bull head are famous. They were exported up to Etruria (Italy). Works, unearthed from Altıntepe excavations, are exhibited in The Museum of Anatolian Civilizations in Ankara today. Mama Hatun Hostel and Tomb, which are constructed in 13th Century, are located in Tercan county, bounded to Erzincan. Furthermore, Kemah Castle, located in Kemah county, Gülabi Bey Mosque, located in the county center, Tomb of Melik Ghazi from Mengücük Oğulları, constructed in 1191 in the entrance of county are the worth seeinghistoricalstructures. Mineralwaterandalsothermal

Altıntepe - Erzincan

springs, which are important in terms of health tourism, are located in Ekşisu location in 13 km east of Erzincan.

Mamahatun Caravanserai and Tomb-Erzincan

Erzurum

ERZURUM

Furthermore, Girlevik Waterfall, located in 30 km. southern-east of the city, is the popular touristic and resort place of the region with its natural beauty and coolness. Moreover, Erzincan Museum is located within Cultural Center in the city. Excavations, which are made on the tumulus around Erzurum, show that first settlements here date back B.C. 4000 years. City enters under rule of respectively Hittites after B.C. 1500, Urartians in B.C. 9th Century, Persians in B.C. 546; Alexander the Great Empire in B.C. 333, and after Alexander the Great Empire is broken into pieces in A.D. 323. Armenia Kingdom is established in this region of Anatolia, which falls to the share of Seleuceians. Later on, region is ruled respectively by Romans, Byzantines, Sasanians, Arabians and again Byzantines. Saltukoğulları Beylic is established in Erzurum region after Battle of Malazgirt in 1071. Anatolian Seljuks Sultan Rükneddin Süleyman II (1196-1204) brings an end to Saltukoğulları Beylic in 1201. Erzurum, which is exposed to Mongol invasion in 1243 and Timur invasion in 1402, witnesses combats between Karakoyunlular and Akkoyunlular. Finally, it is included into Ottoman lands in 1514. Erzurum remains under Russian invasion (February-1916- March 1917) during The First War. Erzurum hosts National Congress, organized in July 23, 1919 – August 17, 1919 in the first years of Independence War. We can list the historical structures, located in the city, as follows. Erzurum Castle belongs to Byzantine period and is constructed during the period of emperor Theodosios II (408-450) in 415 and undergoes repair repeatedly in the next periods. Only citadel is standing. Tepsi Minaret, which is constructed between 1124-1132 during the period of Saltukoğulları Beylic, is located within the castle. Yakutiye Madrasah, which is one of the most beautiful works in Erzurum, is constructed by the order of Hoca Cemalettin Yakut in 1315 during the period of İlhanlılar; Çifte Minaret Madrasah is also constructed during the period of İlhanlılar between 1285-1290 years. Furthermore, Ahmediye Madrasah, which is stated in its epigraph that it is constructed by Ahmet, son of Ali, in 1314, is among the important madrasah structures in Erzurum. Ulu Mosque is constructed by the order of Mehmet Kızılaslan in 1179 during the period of Saltukoğulları. Lala Mustafa Pasha Mosque is constructed by Sinan the Architect by the order of Beylerbeyi Lala Mustafa Pasha in 1562. Murat Pasha Mosque is constructed by the order of Kuyucu Murat Pasha in 1572. Furthermore, Ali Pasha Mosque, constructed by the order of Ali Pasha in 1595; 1558 dated Ayas Pasha Mosque, constructed by the order of Ayas Pasha; Bakırcı Mosque, constructed by the order of Mustafa Ağa in 1720; Caferiye Mosque, constructed by the order of Haci Cafer in 1645; İbrahim Pasha Mosque, constructed by the order of Governor Hacı İbrahim Pasha in 1748; Gürcü Mehmet Pasha Mosque, constructed by the order of Gürcü Mehmet Pasha in 1648; and Three large tombs, composed of Emir Saltuk Large Tomb, belonging to 12th century and two other large tombs, located near it and belonging to 14th century, 1308 dated Karanlık Large Tomb; Mehti Abbas Large Tomb, belonging to 15th Century; Gümüşlü Large Tomb, Cimcime Sultan Large Tomb and Rabia Hatun Large Tomb, belonging to 14th Century; Ahil Baba Large Tomb, belonging to 16th Century, 1561 dated Üstem Pasha Bazaar, Gümrük Hostelry, Kamburoğlu Hostelry, Lala Pasha Hamam, Boyahane Hamam, Çifte Göbek Hamam, Murat Pasha Hamam are some of the other old works, located in Erzurum. Moreover, Erzurum Museum, in which archaeological and ethnographic works are exhibited, Atatürk House Museum, and 23 July Congress Hall Museum are the museums, located in the city.

View from Erzurum

Kars

KARS

It is said that name of Kars is originated from Karsak Turkish clan, who comes from north and settles here. Region is ruled by Urartians from B.C. 9th Century to B.C. 6th Century. Later on, city enters under the rule of respectively Scythians, Persians, Alexander the Great; Seleucians in B.C. 189 and it is captured by Sasanians in A.D. 430 and then Arabians in 716. Caliph declares Sembad, son of Bagratid Ashot, as patrician of Christians in 861, and II. Ashot, son of Sembad, gets title of king from caliph in 886, Kars becomes center of a Bagratid Dynasty in 928. Bagratids move their center to Ani in 962. Kars enters under rule of Byzantines in 1045; Seljuks in 1080. Later on, city remains under the rule of respectively Saltukoğulları, Mongolians, Karakoyunlular, Akkoyunlular and it is included into Ottoman lands in 1534. Kars passes under the control of Russians at the end of Ottoman Russia War in 1878. It witnesses Russian invasion for 40 years between 1878-1918. As city witnesses great attacks throughout the history, it is destroyed substantially, therefore, old structures are not seen in the city. We can list important historical works in Kars as follows: Kars Castle, located on a hill in the north of city, is constructed during the period of Saltukoğulları in 1152 and it is composed of two sections as citadel and bailey. It is the oldest Turkish Castle in Anatolia. Castle is destroyed due to wars continuously. However, it undergoes repair during the reign of Kanuni Sultan Süleyman and in 19th Century. Church, which is constructed for the name of 12 apostles by Bagratids in 937, is turned into the mosque in 1579 and called Kümbet Mosque. Evliya Mosque and Yusuf Pasha Mosque, constructed in 1579, Stone Bridge, belonging to the period of III. Murat, İlbeyi and Cuma Baths, belonging to 18th Century, are some of the other old structures in the city. Kars Museum, containing archaeological and ethnographic works, attracts attention especially in terms of richness of ethnographic works.

View from Erzurum

ANİ

It is a castle city, surrounded with walls and located within boundaries of Kars Province, Arpaçay County, and in the border of Armenia. Bagatid Dynasty moves its capital city from Kars to Ani under the management of king III. Ashot in 962. Great public works are started in Ani city. City is furnished with architectural structures. City enters under Byzantine rule in 1044. Ani is captured and destroyed by Alpaslan in 1064. Ani City passes under the control of Georgians in 1124; Mongolians in 1239 and it is destroyed substantially at the end of earthquake, occurred in 1319. City is exposed to Timur invasions in 1360 and appears like a small village in 16th Century. Citadel inside Ani city is constructed in A.D. 5th century. Walls, surrounding the original city, are constructed subsequently in 10th century. There are seven big gates on city walls. These gates are called Aslanlı Gate, Kars Gate, Hıdırellez Gate, Acemoğlu Gate, Tatarcık Deresi Gate, Divin Gate, and Suyolu Gate. We can list remains of important structures inside the city from north to south as f ollows: Apostles Church (Surp Hovhannes), constructed in 10th century, Ateşgede(the place worshipping for fire) (Gheber Ghebre temple), belonging to 5th century; Ba gradits Palace, constructed in 1092, King Gagik Church, Church, which is constructed as Patriarchate in 1031 and turned into Hostel by Seljuks, Ebul Muammeran Mosque, constructed in 1365, Surp Krikor Abugamrents Church, constructed in 994; Great Cathedral, constructed by I. Gagik in 1001 and turned into the mosque under the name of Fethiye Mosque after conquest of Ani city by Alpaslan in 1064, Keseli Church (Surp Pırgich Church), constructed in 1035; Surp Krikor Lusavorich Church, constructed in 1215; Maiden's Monastery (Virgins Monastery), constructed in 13th century; Ulu Mosque (Menüçehr Mosque), constructed in 1072; II. Ashot Church, constructed between 914-929, Citadel and Maiden's Castle and also Bridge, connecting two sides to each other on Arpaçay Stream, are some of important and old structure remains in Ani ancient city.

İshakpaşa Palace

İSHAKPAŞA PALACE / DOĞUBEYAZIT

Ishakpasa Palace is constructed onto the terrace, constituted on a mountainous area, dominating the lowland in 5 km. east of Doğubeyazıt County, bounded to Ağrı Province. It is understood from the existing epigraph that the construction of palace is started in 1684 and the construction of palace is completed by Ishak Pasha in 1785. Palace is surrounded with high walls and it is in the position of the castle. It is entered into the palace, which is composed of interior and exterior courtyards, through a monumental gate, opening to the east. All of the service buildings, located in the exterior courtyard, are destroyed completely. It is entered into the interior courtyard through a second monumental gate. Structures, which are in the left side of such courtyard, are in ruined position. Selamlık structures, mosque and tomb adjacent to the mosque are located in the right side. It is entered into Harem from a third monumental gate in the second courtyard. Besides rooms; kitchen, storeroom, bakery and bath are located in Harem section. Second floor of harem section with two floors is destroyed completely. Stonework decorations on the monumental gates remind Seljuks period.

Van Castle

VAN

Excavations and researches, which are made around Van Province, show that first settlements here date back B.C. 4000 years. It is seen that region, containing around Lake Van, are ruled respectively by Hurrians by beginning from B.C. 2000, Hittites in B.C. 1500, Assyrians in B.C. 1200. Urartians dominate Van and its surrounding between B.C. 860-580. The capital city is Tushpa. Tushpa is the current Van Castle. King I. Sardur (B.C.840-830) transforms Urartians into a state and establishes Tushpa city and he causes others write the epigraph, explaining how he establishes the state, into the wall of bastion in the northern side of the castle. After Urartians, establishing a powerful state and dominating the region for about 300 years, go out of existence in B.C. 585, region is ruled respectively by Medians, Persians, Alexander the Great, Seleucians and finally Romans in B.C. 66. While this region witnesses Sasanian, Arabian, Byzantine and Armenian conflicts after Romans, region is ruled by Seljuks in 1064. Region, entering under Anatolian Seljuks rule in 1232, is exposed to Mongol invasion in 1243. Later on, region enters under rule of İlhanlılar, Karakoyunlular, Timur Empire, Akkoyunlular and finally Ottomans (1548) in 15th Century. Van Castle, which is surrounded with walls, is constructed in Urartian period and castle, which is destroyed from time to time and repaired repeatedly in the subsequent periods, is also used and undergoes repair for many times in Ottoman period. Structures such as mosque, madrasah, military headquarters and stores, belonging to Ottoman period are located in the castle. Van ancient city is situated in the castle foot. Ulu Mosque, belonging to 14th Century, Kaya Çelebi Mosque, constructed in 1660, Hüsrev Pasha Mosque, constructed in 1567 and remains of some old structures are located here. Ancient Van, which is destroyed substantially during The First World War (1914-1918), is abandoned and current Van city is settled in the region, called "Bağlar". There is a rich museum, which is required to be visited and in which especially archaeological works, local ethnographic works of Urartian period are exhibited, in Van. Furthermore, there are many Urartian Castle and settlement places in Van region.

AKDAMAR / *Ahdamar*

Ahtamar Island is located within the bay in south-east direction of Lake Van and in 4 km. far from the coast and it is the biggest island within the lake. The oldest settlements in the Island, belong to Armenian Period. It is said that first settlements belong to A.D. 4th Century. Island was the capital city of Armenian Kingdom once upon a time. Island was managed by Reshtuni Family and a monastery was constructed by the order of Tehodor Reshtuni in 653. Armenian patricians were residing in this island between 924-959. Palace, church and port were constructed here by the order of Vaspurakan king I. Gagik between 915-921. Only standing church can reach today among these works. Structure, named as "Holy Cross Church" and reaching today in standing position, is constructed by king I. Gagik and clergyman-architect Manuel between 915-921. Red sand Stones, used in the construction of church, is brought from Diyarbakır. Later on, outbuildings are constructed and church is extended. The church has a plan with four wings and cross shaped. Main place is covered with a cylindrical body and conical roof. Bell tower is added into south side of the church in 1900. Wall pictures (frescos) are still noticed under whitewash inside the church. Scenes, received from the holy books (Adam, Eve, David etc.) and king Gagik and his Family and saint reliefs are engraved onto the exterior walls of the church. These frescos and reliefs are restored by Armenian businessmen Gulbenkyan Foundation in 1963. Repair works are also started in the church in 2006 and it is opened as monumental museum for public visits in March, 2007. 1358 dated Halime Hatun Large Tomb, belonging to Karakoyunlular period, is located in Gevaş, which is located next to Ahtamar Island. Some church and monastery remains are also situated in the other small islands other than Ahtamar Island in Van Lake.

Akdamar (Van)

Ahlat

AHLAT

It is thought that Ahlat, located in the northern-west shore of Van Lake, is established by Urartians, establishing a state in Eastern Anatolia between B.C. 680-550. However, Ahlat gains great importance because it is one of the first places, in which Turks enter into Anatolia and settle after 1071 and thus, it takes its place in the history. Great Seljuks Sultan gives the region to Seljuks emirs Sökmen Bey in 1100. Thus, Ahlatşahlar Beylic is established in 1100 and its center is Ahlat. Later on, Ahlat and its region are ruled respectively by Ayyubids in 1207, Celaleddin Harzemşah in 1229. After Mongol invasion in 1243, it is ruled respectively by İlhanlılar, Karakoyunlular in 1336, then it is invaded by Timur, after it is ruled by Akkoyunlular in 1467 and finally, it is included into Ottoman lands by Yavuz Sultan Selim in 1514. Although Ahlat is a small county, it has a rich historical and cultural heritage. New Castle, which is constructed in Ottoman period, is located in the shore of lake and Old Castle is located on a hill, in the slightly inland. Old structures in Ahlat are ruinous and most of them are destroyed. Ahlat is known with its ancient graves and large tombs. Cemeteries and large tombs are protected and reach today. Meydanlık Cemetery, Castle Cemetery, Merkez Cemetery, Kırklar Cemetery, Kadı Cemetery are some of these cemeteries. Grave stones in these cemeteries, dated as 12th-15th centuries, exhibit the most beautiful models of Seljuks stonework. Ahlat has extremely authentic works in terms of its large tombs. Usta Şakirt Large Tomb, belonging to end of 13th century, 1275 dated Hasan Aka Large Tomb, 1279 dated Hüseyin Timur Large Tomb, 1281 dated Boğatay Aka - Şirin Hatun Large Tomb, 1306 dated Emir Ali Large Tomb, 1377 dated Erzen Hatun Large Tomb, 1481 dated Emir Bayındır Large Tomb are some of them. Archaeological works, Seljuks and Ottoman period ait ethnographic works, belonging to Paleolithic, Ancient Bronze, Urartian, Roman, Byzantine periods are exhibited in Ahlat Museum and Seljuks period "Ahlat Gravestones" are exhibited in the garden of museum.

HARPUT / Mamuret-ül-Aziz / Elazığ

Elazığ city is established in 19th century. Reşid Mehmet Pasha, taking Office as army marshal and expanded state governor in Harput in 1834, has managerial center of city moved into the place called Mezraa in the lowland in 5 km. far from Harput, and has barracks and government building constructed. Thereupon, city is moved here. Name of city is Mezraa during the reign of Sultan Abdülaziz in 1862 and it is changed as Mamuret-ül-Aziz. Later on, this name is shortened as Elaziz and it is called Elazığ with a law, enacted in 1937 in Republic period. Harput is established in a place, which is dominating the lowland and easy to defend in 1280 m height in 5 km. north of Elazığ. First settlement started in Harput since prehistoric ages and name of Harput passes as Harputa in Hittite cuneiform script documents. Hurrians dominate the region at the beginning of B.C. 2nd thousand, and they leave the region to Hittites in B.C. 1400. After Hittite Empire is destroyed in B.C. 1183, region is ruled firstly by Assyrians, then Urartians, and then Persians in B.C. 546, and it is also ruled respectively by Macedonians, Seleucians, Sasanians, Romans and Byzantines. Harput is exposed to Arabian invasions in 7th Century. Harput remains under rule of Umayyad and Abbasid and then Artuqid for short period and remains under Seljuks rule for long period. It is exposed to Mongol invasion in 1243. Later on, Harput is ruled firstly by Dulkadiroğulları Beylic and then Karakoyunlular and Akkoyunlular. Harput enters under Ottoman rule certainly in 1515. Harput Castle is located in southern-east of the city. Castle, which is supposed to be constructed by Urartians in B.C. 9th Century, undergoes repairs substantially in Artuqids, Dülkadiroğulları and Akkoyunlular period. The Virgin Mary church is situated in the east of castle. Old works in Harput belong to Artuqid, Seljuk, Akkoyunlu and Ottoman periods. Harput Ulu Mosque, reaching today in a standing position, is constructed by the order of Artuqid Sultan Fahreddin Karaaslan in 1156. Esadiye (Aslanlı) Mosque, which is known to be constructed by Melik Esad in 12th Century, Alacalı Mosque, which is supposed to be constructed in Artuqid period in 1202-1204 and undergoes repair in Ottoman period, Sara Hatun Mosque, constructed by the order of Sara Hatun, who is mother of Akkoyunlu Sultan Uzun Hasan in 1463, Kurşunlu Mosque, constructed in Ottoman period in 1738 are among the important mosque structures in the city. Besides mosques, there

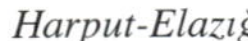

Harput-Elazığ

Arap Baba Tomb-Elazığ

are tombs and small mosques. 1185 dated Ahi Musa Small Mosque and Tomb, Mansur Baba Tomb, belonging to 12th Century, 1279 dated Seljuks period Arap Baba Small Mosque and Tomb, Beşik Baba Tomb and ruinous baths are also some of the other old structures. Furthermore, Harput Museum, which is located in Harput, is one of the places, which are required to be visited. As current Elazığ city is a new city, old structures are not seen here mostly. However, Archaeological and Ethnography Museum, in which rich archaeological and ethnographic works are exhibited, are located in Elazığ city.

Crooked Minaret-Elazığ

Malatya

MALATYA

Name of Malatya is the transformed form of Melitene name, which is the name of this region in the ancient age, in the course of time. Settlement into current Malatya starts after Reforms Period and Malatya could be a province just in Republic period. Ancient Malatya is in the place where current Battalgazi County is located in 9 km. far from current Malatya and it maintains to be city center as Ancient Malatya until 1938. Researches, which are made around Malatya, show that first settlements here date back the Neolithic period. Region is ruled by Hittites in B.C. 1500. After Hittite Empire goes out of existence in B.C. 1183, after this region is ruled firstly by Assyrians and then Urartians, again Assyrians and then respectively Persians, Macedonians Seleucians, Kingdom of Cappadocia and Kingdom of Pontus, it enters under the rule of Roman Empire in B.C. 66. Malatya, remaining within Eastern Roman boundaries, is exposed of invasions of Sasanians in 6th Century, Arabians in 7th Century. Even though Abbasids dominate the city at the end of 8th Century, city passes under the control of Byzantines again 10th century. Later on, after rule of Danişmedoğulları, Anatolian Seljuks, and Mongol invasion, and the city is ruled by İlhanlılar, Memluks, Dülkadiroğulları Beylic and Ottomans. After invasion of Timur, city goes between Ottomans and Memluks and finally it is included into Ottoman lands certainly in 1516. As current Malatya is a new city, old structures are not seen here mostly. Old structures are located in Malatya ancient city in Battalgazi county. Among these structures, Ulu Mosque, constructed by the order of Yakuboğlu Mansur during the period of Seljuks Sultan I. Alaeddin Keykubat in 1224, 1393 dated Melik Sunullah Mosque, 1376 dated Şehabiye-i Kübra Madrasah, Akminare Mosque, constructed by the order of Zaim Yusufoğlu Hikmet Bey in 1573, Sütlüminare Mosque, constructed at the end of 16th century; Karahan Mosque, constructed by the order of Hüsrev Bey, son of Malatya colonel Abdullah in 1583, 1563 dated Emir Ömer Small Mosque, and also Emir Ömer Tombs, Siddi Zeynep Large Tomb, Üçkardeşler Tomb, Hacı Nefise Hatun Tomb, Kanlı Large Tomb and 1637 dated Silahtar Mustafa Pasha Hostel are some of

Arslantepe - Malatya

the other works in Malatya. Ancient Malatya Castle is constructed during the period of Roman Emperor Titus (A.D. 79-81). Castle undergoes repair during the period of emperor Iustinianos in 532 in Byzantine period. Castle is destroyed by Sasanians in 575 and Byzantines in 934 and castle is repaired during the period of Byzantine emperor Dukas in 1059-1067, and also during the period of II. Kılıçaslan in 1181 again and it is surrounded with double row wall. There is a rich museum, in which archaeological and ethnographic works, belonging to various periods, are exhibited, in New Malatya city.

Local Products-Malatya

A General View from Gaziantep Museum

GAZİANTEP

Gaziantep is an industrial city. The archaeological researches, which are made around Gaziantep, show that first settlements here date back B.C. 5000. It is seen that region is ruled firstly by Hurrians at the beginning of B.C. 2nd thousand and then Mitannians and Hittites. Hittite Art continues for about 500 years in Late Hittite City States, which are established in the region after Hittite Empire is destroyed in B.C. 1200. However, region is ruled firstly by Assyrians by beginning from B.C. 9th century and then respectively Urartians and Medians. Region, entering under rule of Persians in B.C. 546, Macedonians in B.C. 333 and then Seleucians, and Roman Empire in B.C. 69, remains within boundaries of Eastern Roman Empire after Roman Empire is divided into two pieces in 395. Gaziantep and its surrounding witness the wars, which are made between Umayyad, Abbasid, Muslim Turkish states, Byzantines and Crusaders by beginning from 7th century. It is exposed to Mongol invasion in 13th century. Later on, city is ruled by Dülkadiroğulları, even if Timur invasion occurs for some time, and then city is ruled again by Dülkadiroğulları and finally, it is included into Ottoman lands certainly in 1516. Name of city passes as "Ayıntab" for the first time during Crusades. Antep name is the transformed form of Ayıntab in the course of time. City is called Gaziantep in 1921. A watch tower was located on a natural hill in the middle of city in Roman Age. Byzantine period emperor Iustinianos I. (527-565) gets extant Gaziantep Castle constructed here. Castle was fortified with some towers and also repaired in Memluks and Ottoman period. Various old structure remains are available in the castle. As it is ancient city, there are ancient historical structures such as a lot of mosques, small mosques, bazaar, covered bazaar, market, hostelry, hostel, hamam, tomb, fountain in Gaziantep. The oldest mosque in the city is Boyacı Mosque, which is constructed in Memluks period in 1357. Ömeriye Mosque, Alinacar Mosque, Eyüboğlu Mosque, Kılıçoğlu Mosque, Kozluca Mosque, Ahmet Çelebi Mosque, Hüseyin Pasha Mosque are some of them. Attractive feature of mosques in Gaziantep is that balconies in the minarets have roof. The most important place, which is required to be vis-

Gaziantep Castle

ited in Gaziantep, is Gaziantep Museum, having the richest mosaics in the worldwide. These mosaics belong to Zeugma ancient city, which is rescued from submerging in Birecik Dam. Various mythological scenes are depictured in these mosaics, belonging to Roman Age. Mosaics, fresco and the other archaeological works, unearthed from rescuing excavations in Zeugma, are exhibited in the additional museum building, constructed with two floors. Works, belonging to prehistoric ages, works, belonging to Late Hittite, Assyrian, Urartian, Classical, Hellenistic, Roman, Byzantine and Ottoman periods are exhibited in the old museum building. Hasan Süzer Ethnography Museum, in which ethnographic works are exhibited, is also among the places, which are required to be visited in the city.

Gaziantep

Fish Lake-Şanlıurfa

ŞANLIURFA

Round structures, belonging to B.C. 10 500, are unearthed in the excavations, which are made in Göbekli Hill around Urfa. Thus, Urfa has a history for twelve thousand five hundred years as of now and also is also known as "City of Prophets" because prophets such as Abraham, Ayoub and Shoaib live in this city. Urfa is established on the territories, called "Fertile Crescent" in the archaeological literature because it is a region, from which culture and citizenship is spread into the worldwide. Region is ruled firstly by Hurrians in B.C. 1500 and then respectively Mitannians, Hittites, Assyrians, Urartians, Medians, Persians, Alexander the Great and Seleucians. Edessa name is used instead of Urhay/Urfa by beginning from Seleucians period. Syrians establish Osrhoene Kingdom, whose capital city is Urfa in B.C. 132. Urfa becomes colony of Roman Empire during the period of emperor Caracalla (211-217) in A.D. 216. After Roman Empire is divided into two pieces in 395, Urfa remains within Eastern Roman Empire lands. Urfa goes between Arabians and Eastern Romans by beginning from 640. City is ruled by Seljuks in 1087. Urfa Shire is established in 1098 during I. Crusade. Later on, city is ruled respectively by Artuqidsr, Ayyubids and Anatolian Seljuks. After Mongol, Timur invasions, Memluk and Akkoyunlu rules continue. Urfa is included into Ottoman lands in 1516. We can list some of the important historical works in the city as follows: Urfa Castle is constructed in Seleucians period and as it is destroyed in the subsequent periods, it is reconstructed in Abbasids period in 814. Castle undergoes repair in Ayyubids, Memluks, Akkoyunlular and Ottoman period. It is stated in the epigraph, on two columns with Corinthian head in the castle that these columns are erected between 240-242. Furthermore, these columns are subject to the myth, causing the constitution of Sacred Fish Lake in Urfa. The structure, whose construction date is not known certainly, and which is transformed into the church in

A General View from Şanlıurfa

5th Century while it is an old panteist temple or synagogue, and named as Red Church as it is constructed from the red marble, is turned into the mosque under the name of Ulu Mosque after Arabian invasion in 7th Century. Semi Dome, Halil-ür Rahman Mosque, constructed in 1211, Halil-ür Rahman Lake, Rıdvaniye Mosque, constructed in 1736, Ayn-ı Zeliha Lake, Mevlüdü Halil Mosque, cave, in which Prophet Abraham was born, Hasan Padishah Mosque, constructed in 1499, are located around Sacred Fish Lake, which is the symbol of Urfa. Moreover, Nimetullah Mosque (Ak Mosque), constructed in 1500, Eski Ömeriye Mosque, constructed in 1301, 1709 dated Yusuf Pasha Mosque and historical hostelries, hamams, madrasahs, bazaars, churches, constructed during Ottoman period and Urfa houses and residences are the other important architectural structures in the province. Şanlıurfa Museum, in which archaeological and ethnographic works are exhibited, is among the places, which are required to be visited in the city. Also, Ataturk Dam, which is the pride source of our country, is located within boundaries of Şanlıurfa province, with its new name, which is the center of GAP (The Southeastern Anatolia Project).

HARRAN

History of Harran, which is located in 47 km south of Şanlıurfa and known with local conic houses, date back very ancient ages. Name of Harran passes in the tablets with cuneiform scripts in B.C. 2000. Moreover, it is said that Prophet Abraham lives in this city for a time before he goes to Paletsine. Old sources mention about existence of Sin Temple in Harran. City is ruled by Assyrians in B.C. 9th Century. Roman emperor Theodosius gets Sin Temple destroyed in A.D. 382. Church is constructed here in 5th Century. Iustinianos (527-565) renews walls, surrounding the city, in 6th century. There are 187 bastions and seven gates on the wall in the length of 4 km. Five of these gates are visible. Musul Gate is located in the east; Halep Gate is located in the west; Aslanlı Gate is located in the north; Rakka and Roman Gate are located in the south. Furthermore, palace, which is constructed during the period of Umayyad sultan II. Mervan, is located with-

Views from Harran

in the citadel in the southern-east of the wall. II. Mervan (744-750) makes Harran the capital city of Umayyads. Ulu mosque, madrasah, bath and hospital are located within the social complex, which is constructed by the order of II. Mervan again in Umayyad period in the northern-east side of the city. Ruinous walls of mosque and its minaret with square body in the form of tower is standing today. It is known that this tower, belonging to older periods, is used as observatory for watching sun, moon and stars on the sky. University, established in Harran during the period of Abbasids (750-1258), has a great fame. Harran, remaining under the rule of various Islamic states until 1260, is exposed to Mongol blockade and invasion and city is burned and destroyed in this date. Harran is included into Ottoman Empire lands as a result of Mercidabik War, which is made with Memluk State in 1516. A tumulus, dating back B.C. 3000 years, is located in the middle of Harran. Archaeological excavations here are carried out by Dr. Nurettin Yardımcı.

Mardin

MARDİN

Researches, which are made around Mardin, show that first settlements here date back B.C. 4000 years. Region is ruled firstly by Hurrians, Mitannians, Hittites, by beginning from B.C. 2000, and respectively by Assyrians in B.C. 1200, Urartians in B.C. 9th Century. While city is ruled respectively by Persians, Macedonians, Seleucians, Romans, Sasanians, Byzantines; Arabians in 7th Century, Hamdani Dynasty in 9th Century, Seljuks in 11th Century and then Artuqids, İlhanlılar, Karakoyunlular, Akkoyunlular, Mardin is included into Ottoman lands just in 1517. As for name of Mardin, Ammianus Marcellinus, living in A.D. 4th century, mentions about that there is a castle, which is called Mazide, here and Syrians call this castle as Marde, Arabians call it as Maridini. Mardin name must be the changed form of these words. Mardin, having a rich historical and cultural heritance, is declared as an urban site area and it is in the position of an unique outdoor museum "museum city". We can list some of the old works in the city, as follows: Mardin Castle is constructed by Hamdanians Family, which is an Arabian dynasty, in 975 -976. Castle, which is located on a rocky hill in the height of 1180 / 1200 m., is also famous owing to being a castle, which is very difficult to be captured due to its position. Only some part of walls reaches today. Some castle remains belonging to Artuqid and Akkoyunlu period are situated in the castle. Ulu Mosque, which is constructed during the period of Artuqid sultan Necmettin İlgazi in 1170, attracts attention especially with various decorations on it and minaret with scripts. Şehidiye Mosque is constructed by Melik Mansur Nasreddin in 1214, its minaret, which is added in 1916, is attractive. Melik Mahmud Mosque, which is constructed by the order of Artuqid Melik Mahmud in 1367, 1314 dated Latifiye Mosque and 1347 dated Hamidiye Mosque, Reyhaniye Mosque and Arabian Mosque, belogning to 16th Century, Zairi Mosque, belonging to 17th Century, Hacı Ömer Mosque, belonging to 18th Century are some of the other mosques in the city. Madrasahs constitute the most important works in the city. Zinciriye Madrasah is constructed by the order of Artuqid Melik Necmeddin İsa in 1385 and madrasah with two floors, is composed of court, mosque, tomb and other sections. Although construction of Kasımiye Madrasah is started at the end of Artuqids period, it is called with this name because it is completed during the period of Kasım (1487-1502), son of Cihangir in Akkoyunlular period. Madrasah with two floors is composed of court, mosque, tomb. Rıdvaniye Madrasah, which is also known with the names of Hatuniye and Sitti Radviyye Madrasah, is constructed by the order of Artuqid sultan Kudbeddin İlgazi between 1176-1185. Madrasah with two floors is composed of court with sheds and cloisters and mosque and tomb. Şehidiye Madrasah, which is constructed by the order of Artuqid Necmeddin Ghazi between 1239-1259, gives the scheme of a madrasah, having a small mosque with iki naves and with the court with cloisters and two sheds. The most important structure, belonging to the Christianity period, in Mardin is Deyrülzafaran Monastery in 5 km. far from the city. Monastery is the religious center of Ancient Syrian community. Syrians regard themselves as the first Christian people. Monastery is estab lished at the end of A.D. 4th Century. It is composed of structures with three floors, surrounding a rectangular interior courtyard. It reaches its current situation with outbuildings, which are made in the various periods and undergoes repairs in 18th Century. There are three churches and chapel, Cemetery of Saints, containing grave of 52 Syrian patricians, Ceremony section within the monastery and also monastery has a guesthouse. Besides these structures, a lot of old mosque, madrasah, hamam, hostelry, small dervish lodge, tomb, fountain, monastery, church structure and Mardin houses are the other important structures, which are required to be visited, in the city. Mardin Museum, serving in an old structure, is among the places, which are required to be visited. Midyat county, bounded to Mardin, is an important county, which is required to be visited, be cause of its architectural buildings and silver engraving.

Deyrülzafaran Monastery-Mardin

HASANKEYF

Hasankeyf, which is bounded to Batman Province, is a county, which is located in the southern shore of Dicle River. Its old name is Hısn - Kayfa. Word of Hısn means castle or fortress, Kayfa means rock. It is called Hasankeyf in the Ottoman period. Hasankeyf, which is a very old settlement place with its cave houses, which is an accommodation place in the waterfront on the trade road, going to east in the ancient age, was a settlement place on the eastern boundary of Romans. After rule of Romans, city is ruled respectively by Byzantines, Abbasids, Hamdanians, Mervanians and finally Artuqids in 1102. Hasankeyf becomes the capital city of Artuqid Beylic. While region is ruled by Ayyubids in 1231, Mongols capture and destroy the city in 1260. Later on, even though Karakoyunlular and Safavids dominate the city, it is included into Ottoman lands in 1517. City lives its most prime period during the period of Artuqids. We can list the old structures in the city, as follows: Hasankeyf Castle is 100 m height from Dicle River. Castle is constructed during the period of Roman emperor Iulianus (361-363) and Iovianus (363-364) in 363, outbuildings and gates are constructed in the period of Artuqids and Ayyubids. There are many structure and structure remains within the castle. Ulu Mosque is constructed in Ayyubids period in 1325, mosque undergoes repair in 1394 according to the epigraph, detected here. Great Palace ruins are located in the bottom section of Ulu Mosque. Although El-Rızk Mosque, which is located in the northern-west of the city, is ruinous, its magnificent minaret reaches today in standing position. According to detected epigraph, mosque is constructed by the order of Ayyubids sultan Süleyman in 1409. Süleymaniye Mosque, which is also constructed by the order of Sultan Süleyman in 1407, is ruinous and only its minaret is standing. Furthermore, there are ruined mosque, hamam madrasah, palace, wall and houses inside the city. It is understood from the epigraph that ruined bridge on Dicle River, is constructed in Artuqids period in 1116 and undergoes repair in Ayyubids period in 1349. Zeynel Bey Tomb, constructed by Akkoyunlu sultan Uzun Hasan for his son, who is died in Otlukbeli War, which he makes with Fatih Sultan Mehmet in 1473 and İmam Abdullah Small Dervish Lodge, constructed in Ayyubids period and in the ruinous position in these days, are located in the opposite side of Dicle River. Hasankeyf is submerged with its historical values, having the cultural heritage, and its settlement places, constituted by caving the rocks due to Ilısu Dam, to be constructed on Dicle River.

Hasankeyf

Diyarbakir City Walls

DİYARBAKIR

It is understood from the findings, which are obtained from the archeological excavations, made on the tumulus in Çayönü that first settlement started around Diyarbakır in the Neolithic period (B.C. 7250- B.C. 6750). The first settlement in Diyarbakır city is in İçkale location in B.C. 2000 and it corresponds to Hurrians period. Mitannians dominate the period by beginning from B.C. 1500. Name of the city is Amidi in Assyrian sources dated B.C. 1300. This name changes and takes the shape of Amid in the course of time. Region is ruled firstly by Hittites by beginning from B.C. 1380 and then Assyrians, Urartians, Persians, Alexander the Great, Seleucians, Partians, Romans in B.C. 69. After Roman Empire is divided into two pieces in 395, Diyarbakır remains within boundaries of Eastern Roman Empire. City is ruled by Arabians in 639, Seljuks in 1085, and then respectively İnaloğulları, Nisanoğulları, Artuqids, Anatolian Seljuks, Timur Empire, Karakoyunlular, Akkoyunlular and finally Ottomans in 1515. The important structure of the city is Diyarbakır Castle, composed of Citadel and Bailey. There are four gates in the citadel, Fetih Gate and Oğrun Gate are opened outside the city, Saray Gate and Küpeli Gate are opened into Bailey, which is the city center. Bailey Walls, which are also including Citadel, are in the length of 5,5 km and it has 82 bastions and four main gates, opening out of wall in the four directions. Dağ Gate (Harput Gate) is opened to the north, Urfa Gate (Greek Gate) is opened to the west, Mardin Gate (Tell Gate) is opened to the south, Yeni Gate (Su or Dicle Gate) is opened to the east. Among the bastions, located on the walls Ulubeden, Yedikardeş and Keçi Bastions are the works of Artuqids. There are many epigraphs, belonging to various periods, on Diyarbakır Walls. Diyarbakır Walls are almost an Epigraph Museum with these rich epigraphs. These epigraphs, bringing light to the history of Diyarbakır, belong to Roman, Byzantine, Abbasid, Seljuk, Artuqid, Ayyubid, Akkoyunlu and Ottoman periods and is in Greek, Latin, Persian and Arabic language. There are many old structures in Diyarbakır, having a long historical past. We can list some of other important architectural structures in the city as follows. When

Diyarbakır

Diyarbakir Castle

Diyarbakır is captured by Arabians in 639, St. Tomas cathedral, located here, is turned into the mosque and called Ulu Mosque. Zinciriye Madrasah is constructed in the southern-west of Ulu Mosque in 1199, Mesudiye Madrasah is constructed in its northern side in 1224. İskender Pasha Mosque, constructed between 1551-1563, Safa Mosque, constructed in 1532, Kara Mosque, constructed by Kara Mustafa Pasha between 1644-1650 years, Kasım Padishah Mosque, constructed in 1500, Kurşunlu Mosque (Fatih Pasha Mosque), constructed by the order of Bıyıklı Mehmet Pasha in 1522, Behram Pasha Mosque, constructed in 1572, Hüsrev Pasha Mosque, constructed between 1522-1528, Melik Ahmet Pasha Mosque, constructed in 1587-1591, Prophet Mosque, constructed in 15th century and also Deliler Hostelry, Hasan Pasha Hostelry, Çifte Hostelry, Melik Ahmet Pasha Bath, Kadı Bath, Diyarbakır Houses and The Virgin Mary Church (Syrian), belonging to 3rd Century, St. George Church and Dicle Bridge, located on Dicle River, are some of the other important old structures in the city. Archeological Museum, in which archaeological and local ethnographic works, belonging to various periods, are exhibited, Cahit Sıtkı Tarancı House, Ziya Gökalp Museum and Command Atatürk Museum are the other places, which are required to be visited in Diyarbakır.

Nemrut (Nimrud)

NEMRUT

Kingdom of Commagene is established at the beginning of B.C. 1st century and it is a kingdom, which goes out of existence by Romans in A.D. 72 and maintains its rule in the region, including current Adıyaman, Gaziantep and Maraş provinces. Its capital city is Arsameia city in the foothills of Mount Nemrut and in the shore of Nymph Stream (Kahta Stream). Other important cities of Kingdom of Commagene are Samosata, Perrhe, Doliche and Germanikeia Kaisareia. Commagene king Antiochus rules between B.C. 62-32 years. Tumulus (grave) of Commagene king Antiochus, located in Mount Nemrut, which is situatede within boundaries of current Adıyaman Province and in 2150 m. height from the sea, is in the shape of a conic hill, constituting stones in the fist size and covers a field in 50 m. height and

in the diameter of 150 m. Tumulus is placed on a rocky hill. It is understood that bones or ashes of King are put into a room, caved into a main rock, and covered with stones in the fist size and a tumulus is constituted. Tumulus must be constructed in the middle of B.C. 1st Century (in B.C. 50) probably. Tumulus, which is protected within Mount Nemrut National Park, is an important archaeological center with its position and mysterious sculptures. Common features of Greco-Pers sculpture art are seen in the sculptures. Furthermore, the natural event, related to sunrise and sunset in the mountain, adds a separate fascinating and mysterious beauty to here. Arsameia ancient city, which is the capital city of Kingdom of Commagene, is located in the shore of Kahta Stream in 26 km. far from Kahta. Old structure remains, a tunnel with arcway and epigraph are seen in the place, which is called Old Castle. The most attractive opus here is high relief opus, showing that Commagene king dressed Mithridates (B.C.109-69) shakes hand with naked Heracles. Cendere Bridge, which is constructed in honour of Roman Empire Septimius Severus and his wife Iulia Domna and their sons Caracalla and Geta in A.D. 198-200, is located on Cendere Stream, which is one branch of Kahta Stream in 3 km far from this ancient city. Woman tumuluses belonging to Commagene Emperial Family are located on Karakuş Hill, in 9 km. far from this bridge. Furthermore, there is a museum, in which archaeological and ethnographic works are exhibited in Adiyaman, on the main road.

KARADE
BULGARİSTAN
YUNANİSTAN
MARMARA DENİZİ
EGE DENİZİ
AKDENİZ
EDİRNE
KIRKLARELİ
TEKİRDAĞ
İSTANBUL
KOCAELİ
İZMİT
SAKARYA
ADAPAZARI
YALOVA
DÜZCE
BOLU
ZONGULDAK
BARTIN
KARABÜK
KASTAMONU
ÇANKIRI
ÇORUM
ÇANAKKALE
BALIKESİR
BURSA
BİLECİK
ESKİŞEHİR
ANKARA
KIRIKKALE
YOZGAT
KÜTAHYA
MANİSA
İZMİR
UŞAK
AFYON
KIRŞEHİR
NEVŞEHİR
AKSARAY
NİĞDE
AYDIN
DENİZLİ
ISPARTA
BURDUR
KONYA
KARAMAN
MUĞLA
ANTALYA
MERSİN
TUZ GÖLÜ
KUZEY KIBRIS TÜRK CUMHURİYETİ
GİRNE
GÜZELYURT
LEFKOŞA
İSKELE
GAZİMAĞUSA
LARNAKA
GAZİBAF
LİMASOL
GÜNEY KIBRIS RUM YÖNETİMİ

Bibliography

Akşit, Oktay	: Likya Tarihi, İstanbul 1967
Akşit, İlhan	: Uygarlıklar Ülkesi Türkiye, Akşit Kültür ve Turizm Yayıncılık , 2003
Akşit,İlhan	: Işık Ülkesi Likia, Akşit Kültür ve Turizm Yayıncılık, İstanbul 1998
Akyıldız, Erhan	: Taş Çağı'ından Osmanlı'ya Anadolu, Milliyet Yayını, İstanbul 1990
Akurgal, Ekrem	: Anadolu Uygarlıkları, Net Turistik Yayınları , İstanbul 1989
Aslanapa Oktay	: Türk Sanatı El Kitabı, İstanbul 1993
Ataman Demir	: Çağlar İçinde Antakya, Akbank Yayınları, İstanbul 1996
Avcıoğlu Doğan	: Türklerin Tarihi, Tekin Yayınevi, İstanbul 1978
Bayburtluoğlu,	: Cevdet : Arkeoloji, Kültür ve Turizm Bakanlığı, Ankara 1982
Belge, Murat	: İstanbul Gezi Rehberi, Tarih Vakfı, 1993
Ceram C. W.	:Tanrıların Vatanı Anadolu, Koza Yayınları, İstanbul 1976
Darga, Muhibbe	: Hitit Sanatı, Akbank Kültür ve Sanat kitapları, İstanbul 1992
Dörtlük, Kayhan	: Perge, Side, Aspendos İstanbul 2006
	Dünden Bugüne İstanbul Ansiklopedisi, Tarih Vakfı Yayını, İstanbul 1994
Erdemgil, Selahattin	: Ephesos, Net Turistik Yayınları, İstanbul 1989
Erhat,Arza	: Karya'dan Pamfilya'ya, 1984
Erhat, Azra	: Mitoloji Sözlüğü, Remzi Kitapevi Yayınları, İstanbul 1972
Erim, T. Kenan	: Aphrodisias, Net Turistik Yayınları, İstanbul 1990
Erzen,Afif	: Doğu Anadolu ve Urartular, Ankara 1984
Freely, John	: Türkiye Uygarlıklar Rehberi, YKY. İstanbul 2003
Işık Adem	: Antik Kaynaklarda Karadeniz Bölgesi, T.T.K.Yayını Ankara 2001
	: İl İl Büyük Türkiye Ansiklopedisi, Milliyet
Kılıçkaya,Ali	: Ayasofya ve Kariye, Dost Turistik Yayınları, İstanbul 2008
Kuban, Doğan	: 100 Soruda Türkiye Sanatı Tarihi, Gerçek Yayınevi, İstanbul 1970
Kunar,Serhat	: Myra, Net turistik Yayınları, İstanbul 1995
Lamec,Jeoffrey	: Kapadokya, Silk Road Turistik Yayınları, İstanbul 2006
Lloyd,Seton	: Türkiye'nin Tarihi, TÜBİTAK Çev. E.Varinlioğlu, Ankara 1997
Müller-Wiener,W.	: Bildlexikon zur Topographie İstanbuls, Tübingen 1977
Orhi, İskender	: Yurdumuzun Öyküsü, İstanbul 1977
Radt, Wolfgang	:Pergamon, Köln 1988
Sözen,Gürol	: Ege'den Akdeniz'e Mavi Yolculuk, Akbank Yayınları, İstanbul 1998
Strabon	: Coğrafya, Anadolu (Kitap XII,XIII,XIV) Çev. A.Pekman,İstanbul 1987
Tanilli, Server	: Uygarlık Tarihi, Alkım Yayınevi, İstanbul 2006
Tuğlacı, Pars	: Osmanlı Şehirleri, Milliyet Yayınları, İstanbul 1985
Umar,Bilge	: Kilikia Bir Tarihsel Coğrafya araştırması ve Gezi Rehberi, İstanbul 2000
Umar Bilge	: Türkiye'deki Tarihsel Adlar, İnkılap Yayınları, İstanbul 1999
Yenen,Şerif	: Anadolu Destanı, İstanbul 1998

Prepared By:

Author	: Ali KILIÇKAYA
Art Selection and Design	: Focus Basım
Photographs	: Erdal YAZICI
Translation	: Expres Tercüme
Colour Seperation and Films	: Eksen Grafik
Printing	: Ebat Basım A.Ş.

ISBN 978-605-5629-20-5

SILK ROAD PUBLICATIONS
Kartaltepe Mah. Yunus Sok. No: 2 - Bayrampaşa - İstanbul
mail. ssilkroad@hotmail.com
Tel: 0212 615 15 01

K
GÜRCİSTAN
TİFLİS
AZERBAYCAN
ERMENİSTAN
ERİVAN
NAHÇIVAN ÖZERK CUMHURİYETİ
İRAN
IRAK
SURİYE
LÜBNAN
SAMSUN
AMASYA
TOKAT
SİVAS
ORDU
GİRESUN
TRABZON
RİZE
ARTVİN
ARDAHAN
KARS
IĞDIR
AĞRI
ERZURUM
BAYBURT
GÜMÜŞHANE
ERZİNCAN
TUNCELİ
BİNGÖL
ELAZIĞ
MALATYA
MUŞ
BİTLİS
VAN
VAN GÖLÜ
HAKKARİ
ŞIRNAK
SİİRT
BATMAN
DİYARBAKIR
MARDİN
ŞANLIURFA
ADIYAMAN
KAHRAMANMARAŞ
GAZİANTEP
KİLİS
OSMANİYE
HATAY
ANTAKYA
HALEP
Halab
HAMAH
Hamath
Batum
KULLANIM ANAHTARI
Otoyollar
İnşa Halinde Otoyollar
Çok Şeritli Yollar
Şehirlerarası Yollar
Asfalt Yollar
Stabilize Yollar
Toprak Yollar
Ham Yollar
Manzaralı Yollar
Demiryolu
Dağ Geçidi
Devlet Sınırları
Gümrük Kapıları
İl Merkezleri
İlçe Merkezleri
TÜRKİYE
FİZİKİ
Ölçek : 1 / 4 500 000
Kilometre 10 0 40 80
Miles 6.2 0 24.8 49.6